WEALTH
BEYOND
WALL STREET

The Roadmap to Wealth and Independence
with Peace of Mind

BRETT KITCHEN & ETHAN KAP

WEALTH BEYOND WALL STREET
The Roadmap to Wealth and Independence with Peace of Mind

© 2015 Brett Kitchen & Ethan Kap.

ISBN 978-1-943277-33-9 paperback

Printed in the United States of America
Year of First Printing: 2015

Cover Design by: Ken Wilcox

DISCLAIMER

While great efforts have been taken to provide accurate and current information regarding the covered material, neither Wealth Beyond Wall Street nor Brett Kitchen or Ethan Kap are responsible for any errors or omissions, or for the results obtained from the use of this information.

The name 'Wealth Beyond Wall Street' is a marketing concept and does not guarantee or imply that you will become wealthy. The act of purchasing any book, course, or financial product holds no such guarantees.

The ideas, suggestions, general principles and conclusions presented here are subject to local, state and federal laws and regulations and revisions of same, and are intended for informational purposes only. All information in this report is provided "as is," with no guarantee of completeness, accuracy, or timeliness regarding the results obtained from the use of this information. And without warranty of any kind, express or implied, including, but not limited to warranties of performance, merchantability, and fitness for a particular purpose. Your use of this information is at your own risk.

You assume full responsibility and risk of loss resulting from the use of this information. Brett Kitchen and/or Ethan Kap and Wealth Beyond Wall Street will not be liable for any direct, special, indirect, incidental, consequential, or punitive damages or any other damages whatsoever, whether in an action based upon a statute, contract, tort (including, but not limited to negligence), or otherwise, relating to the use of this information.

In no event will Brett Kitchen and/or Ethan Kap, Wealth Beyond Wall Street, or their related partnerships or corporations, or the partners, agents, or employees of Brett Kitchen and/or Ethan Kap or Wealth Beyond Wall Street be liable to you or anyone else for any decision made or action taken in reliance on the information in this book or for any consequential, special, or similar damages, even if advised of the possibility of such damages.

A deep-hearted thanks to my fabulous wife Erika who supports me in this amazing venture called life, and my parents Brent and Kathleen Kap who taught me how to live life to the fullest.

Ethan Kap

For my wife, Tiffani, who puts up with endless hours of work and the roller coaster of life married to an entrepreneur, my kiddos who love it when dad gets home, and my parents, Dan and Becky Kitchen who taught me the value of hard work, integrity and good living.

I love you very much.

Brett Kitchen

CONTENTS

Section 4: Examples in Action 123

FOR SKEPTICS ONLY

What does Wealth Beyond Wall Street mean? Here's what it isn't: stuffing your money in a mattress or hunkering down with gold bullion. You don't even have to have a million bucks to be in the club. Becoming wealthy beyond Wall Street means you've started on a low-risk path that will keep your money safely growing over time—guaranteed. Rest assured, for the average American, the dream of becoming a millionaire is not out of reach. In fact, the blueprint is sitting in your hands right now. Here are some of the most common questions people have had before joining the ranks of the wealthy beyond Wall Street.

1. Is it really possible to become wealthy outside of Wall Street?

Actually, it depends. It's not for everyone. Some people are addicted to the ups and downs of the market—and believe it or not, they can't understand how their money can safely grow each and every day regardless of the economy, market or latest bad news on TV. If that's you, then sorry—now's the time to shut the cover on this book and pass it on to someone who wants some security and peace of mind in their financial future.

2. Is it too late for me?

No way! No matter what your age, many of the concepts embraced by Americans getting wealthy outside of Wall Street can be used to grow and safeguard your money for you or your family at any time.

3. Do I have to scrimp and save and basically eat beans and rice in order to grow my money?

Nope. No dietary changes are required to join the club. In fact, once you discover how to Finance Yourself To Wealth™ you may just end up living better, while saving money doing it. There's nothing like living the high life, without the heavy dose of guilt or the pressure of a too-tight budget.

4. Is this just more pop culture investment advice?

This book is for anyone who is sick of the stomach turning ups and downs of what we like to call the "Wall Street Roller Coaster". The principles taught in this book have been around for years. And case studies range from start-up business owners to the average American household and anywhere in between. If you're sick of the status quo and ready to stop drinking the financial guru Kool-Aid, this book is for you.

5. Is this just another financial dead end? How do I know whom to trust?

Fortunately for all of us, the solutions we share with you in this book have been around for over 100 years. In fact, there's a good chance your parents or even grandparents used some of these lost strategies decades ago...you might say we're bringing some financial wisdom back from the dead!

6. Do I need to be a financial whiz?

Not at all. In fact, I think you'll find the whole process refreshingly simple. No monitoring the markets and no complex calculations you need to worry about. Once you get going, becoming wealthy beyond Wall Street can happen almost on autopilot.

Section 1

STATUS QUO KILLERS

"Status quo, you know, that is Latin for 'the mess we're in.'"

— Ronald Reagan

"Bureaucracy defends the status quo long past the time when the quo has lost its status."

—Dr. Laurence J. Peter

Chapter 1

LIES, ADVENTURES, AND KILLING THE STATUS QUO

I was lied to.

Lied to by Washington politicians and the Wall Street propaganda machine.

I started my career helping business owners improve their businesses, increase their cash flow, and grow their profits. It's always exciting to see a client increase their income and create financial independence while working with me. It's one of the most satisfying things I do.

As I started making money, I was shocked at how much I was paying in taxes and immediately looked for as many tax advantages as possible.

With the advice of our CPA, I created an IRA so I could get the deductions and I invested that money in stocks. I was also buying stocks on my own and putting money into several other funds managed by "experts" in the market.

3

Seeing the numbers these investors were quoting, I was excited by the idea that my money could be doubling every seven to eight years...that I could create a million-dollar nest egg and retire wealthy.

That was my plan. Becoming financially independent was always my goal. Having the freedom to choose whether I wanted to work or not. Having the money to travel the world, enjoy a great lifestyle, and provide a financially sound, happy life for my family was my top priority.

I became so excited about the funds I was investing in, I even convinced my own family members to invest their hard-earned money as well.

I listened to many of the major gurus on TV and so called experts on Wall Street and became indoctrinated by the Wall Street propaganda machine. I had been convinced that I needed "aggressive growth" during my younger working years in order to create a nest egg and have a good retirement income in my later years.

The allure of huge returns and people getting rich in the market was blinding.

Like a fool, I didn't look deeper into the Wall Street machine to see who was really making the money.

I didn't realize that I had been indoctrinated, like millions of Americans, to do exactly what the puppet masters in their New York towers wanted us to do.

Who was getting rich in this system?

Was it the average-Joe investor?

Were there really any mutual-fund millionaires?

Or were the guys at the top that managed the funds and charged the fees making all the money?

Like one investor quipped when he visited the yacht club for the fund managers, "Where are all the customers' yachts?"

But I never asked those questions.

I was high on "Hopium." I was hoping that I would get great returns by investing in the market.

Then, at once, it hit.

In a heartbeat, like many Americans, I lost over 35% of the hard-earned money in my stock and IRA accounts.

This was a crushing blow.

I was sick about it.

My dad had warned me, and like a fool I ignored his advice and paid for it.

I felt terrible, but at least I was young and had time to recover. I actually felt even worse for my business partner, Ethan, and his father. Ethan's father lost over half his retirement savings, savings he had worked over 40 years to build.

The timing couldn't have been worse.

He had just recently retired, and now the plans and dreams he and his wife had were dashed. It was financially and emotionally devastating.

The drop happened so fast that there was literally nothing I could do about it.

Many people felt the same way—horrified by seeing their hard-earned money disappear right before their eyes, but powerless to stop it.

Of course, any time a crash happens—(whether it's 1973, 1987, 1997, 2001, 2008, or the next crash)—the money magazines, the talking heads on the TV investing shows, and the brokers on Wall Street all echo the same talking points like a chorus of trained parrots. "Don't sell, don't sell! Hold on to your stocks—they'll come back."

In true fashion, over the course of five or six years the market slowly creeps up, just barely edging back to where it was before the big crash started.

People breathe a collective sigh of relief. "At least my money is back to where it was before!"

It's celebrated, like getting back to even is some kind of great achievement, even though people have lost five years waiting for it to happen.

What no one will tell you is that, on average, over the past 100 years, every 5-7 years there's another market correction or market crash. Often, this takes investors on a yo-yo ride of ups and downs, only to see that, after 10 or 15 years they're about where they started.

The reality is you've lost those five years forever.

But it's worse than that. It's not just about market losses—it's also about taxes. The ravages of taxes can be as deadly to your wealth as market losses, or in some cases, even worse.

In this book, you'll discover the truth about the so-called "tax benefits" of qualified plans (i.e. 401(k)s and IRAs) and it will probably shock you, like it did to me.

After the experience of losing over 35% in my IRA, I said enough.

One of my core values is "Find a Better Way."

So we went on a mission to discover what real-world millionaires were doing to protect their money from taxes, to grow it with good returns and keep it protected while everyone else was getting crushed.

This mission took us on trips across the country and back… giving us exciting experiences we never could have imagined.

One of our first mind-blowing moments happened in a small town outside of Atlanta, Georgia. Ethan and I met with a financial expert who trains thousands of financial advisors across the country on how to help their clients save on taxes.

On a whiteboard, he took us through the numbers and showed us exactly why qualified plans actually cost people *more* in taxes than they saved them.

We were shocked.

Even though I saw the math with my own eyes, I refused to believe it. I said audibly, "That can't be right. Qualified plans are supposed to *save* us taxes, not cost *more* in taxes."

He replied with a laugh, "Don't worry—everyone says the same thing when they see the truth. At first it's hard to believe because you've been sold on the status quo, but the math doesn't lie."

In chapter 5, I'll walk you through the exact same scenario he showed us . . . and I think you'll be as shocked as I was.

Another amazing trip took us to Detroit.

We were picked up in a limousine at the airport and driven through a part of town that looked like a war zone.

This happened during the midst of the Great Recession. Car manufacturers were crushed, Detroit unemployment was off the charts and the city was dying.

The roads were torn up with potholes everywhere. We drove past buildings with windows completely broken out and homeless people on the sidewalks.

The trip took us 30 minutes outside of downtown Detroit to a big office in a small town. Jim's company was making over 50 million per year, and he was a very nice, down-to-earth guy. (So down-to-earth in fact that, after our meeting, he took his motorhome into the mountains for two weeks and left his cell phone at home.)

The "ah-ha" moment here was when he showed us a concept we could use that allows everyday people to earn gains on the same money twice. Banks use fractional reserve lending to earn interest on money they have already lent out. This strategy allowed us to do something similar.

We learned how to finance ourselves in buying cars, homes, vacations, and making other major purchases through a financing system we could control and profit from instead of paying banks to finance those purchases.

It was mind-blowing that everyday people like me could actually be on the right side of the banking equation—paying ourselves interest instead of paying interest to the *banksters*.

"Why haven't we heard this before?" we asked Jim.

His reply made perfect sense. "Who's going to tell you about it? It's not in Wall Street's or Washington's best interest. They control the media—heck, Wall Street *owns* many of the media companies. What do you think they are going to promote?"

You may want to read chapter 9 twice to learn how all this works.

A very strange thing happened on our next trip around the country.

It took us to an estate on a lakefront property down by Florida. Tom and his family had sold their company for over 500 million dollars.

The first house I saw as we pulled into the private lane was large and beautiful, and then I saw the "real" home. (I later found out that the first one was just the guest house.)

Tom and his wife took us on a tour of the property in a golf cart past the pool and down to their boathouse on the lake. There were two boats and two jet skis docked right on the water.

On the way down to the lake, Tom pointed out the graveyard.

"A graveyard?" I asked incredulously.

"Yes," he explained. "After we bought the property, a gardener discovered the graves and came in asking, 'What should I do with the graveyard?'"

The estate was so large that they never knew that there was a small graveyard on it before they bought it. The graves are over 100 years old, so they can't move them!

In my conversations with Tom, he told me something I'll never forget.

He said, "It's no wonder why there is such an incredible difference between the wealthy and the middle class in this country. It's about taxes.

"There are tax-saving advantages and strategies available that are incredibly effective. The problem is that typically, only the ultra-wealthy research and implement them. The middle class gets brainwashed into following the status quo with qualified plans like 401(k)s. They are getting crushed by taxes and never get ahead that way."

In chapter 8, you'll discover a strategy that many experts agree is one of the biggest tax-saving benefits that still exists in the tax code, and you won't have to pay a million-dollar tax attorney to show you how to use it.

One of the most important gems we've learned and share in this book came from a man Ethan and I met at a Chili's restaurant about a mile away from my house.

At the time, I had no idea who Steve was.

But fate brought us together.

He found our business online and was impressed with what we were doing, so he invited us to meet him for lunch. Little did I know that I was in the presence of quite possibly one of the wealthiest men in the world.

After getting to know him and working together for a couple of months, he invited us up to his home to watch a March NCAA basketball tournament game.

When we pulled up, I was shell-shocked.

The house was a palace.

As you walk in through the huge 14-foot hardwood doors onto the circular Travertine landing, there's a beautiful full library on the left with hardwood shelves covering all the walls and a grand piano on the right.

Downstairs there's a dance studio, a full indoor basketball court (my favorite part), a huge theater (including a popcorn maker, my second-favorite part) and outside, a pool with a waterslide.

Then he took us out to the garage. This was truly amazing; we saw his 22-car garage complete with an elevator to move cars from the first floor to the second floor.

Even more impressive were the fully restored classic Shelby Mustangs, Camaros, and dozens of other beautiful classics.

The amazing part of the experiences we had was that the millionaires and multi-millionaires we met weren't really all that affected by the Great Recession.

In fact, Steve was building his multi-million-dollar mansion right in the middle of it—the recession didn't faze him.

Steve took Ethan and me under his wing and mentored us. We spent 2 hours at his office every Thursday afternoon, learning from a man who taught us the strategy we reveal in Chapter 8.

Some people say this sounds "too good to be true" when they first see it—but it is true, and you'll see why in Chapter 8.

=====

We were blessed to go on this amazing journey where we learned from people who created jaw-dropping wealth--safely.

As we picked up these priceless gems from the experts we met on our adventures across the country, we implemented them in our lives.

We tweaked them, refined them, and developed a framework that has been life-changing for us.

It's incredible to see your net worth double or triple in just a few short years; knowing that you are creating a nest egg protected from market downturns that can provide tax-free cash flow without the government's sticky fingers taxing it. It's gratifying to pay off debts and release yourself from those heavy obligations.

It's exciting to be able to take advantage of the strategies typically only used by the wealthiest of people.

We called it the Wealth Beyond Wall Street Framework because that's exactly what we have developed: A process to become a financially independent without gambling in the market or losing money on high-risk investments.

It's not going to happen overnight. It's not a "get rich quick" scheme. But, if you implement these three steps, you can get there.

The first piece of the 4-step Wealth Beyond Wall Street Framework is:

1. **Get your house in order.**

    You can never grow wealthy when you spend more than you make, or you don't control your money.

    It's essential to start with getting organized, making sure you know what money is coming in and where it's going, and having a plan to track spending and get out of debt.

    The second step is:

2. **Build on a steadfast foundation.**

    Every great building is built on a foundation of rock-solid concrete, steel, and rebar.

    No builder would ever dream of building a million-dollar home (or any home, for that matter) on a pile of sand or mud.

    Just like the parable of the wise man and the foolish man— the wise man built on the rock and, when the storm came, his house stood firm. The foolish man built on the sand and, when the storm came, it washed his home away.

    If you build your wealth on a strong foundation, when the storms of stock market crashes hit or the economy goes into recession or depression, you are the wise man with your financial house built on a rock that will not fall.

    Now you can live with a peace of mind difficult to come by in the tumultuous world we live in.

The third step is:

3. **Amplify Your Wealth.**

    This is where it gets really exciting.

This is where you start seeing your wealth grow quickly because you can literally earn interest on the same money twice. (Remember, this is similar to how banks do fractional reserve lending, but *you* get the benefits-not them!)

This is the strategy we used when buying our office building and most recently a lot on our private waterski lake.

In chapters 8, 9, and 10, you'll see all kinds of examples of how you can Amplify Your Wealth by using these strategies.

The last step in the Wealth Beyond Wall Street Framework is:

4. <u>Multiply Your Wealth</u>.

When you multiply your wealth you aren't just getting a few percentage points of growth each year. Now you are seeing your wealth compound in multiples.

The concept behind multiplying your wealth is that you are able to generate capital that becomes a source of passive cash flow you can live off for the rest of your life.

This is where you truly enjoy financial independence, because you now have the freedom to decide what you want to do with your time and talents.

There are several ways you can multiply your wealth. In a later chapter we share several of our favorite and most proven methods of millionaires across the country.

We developed this framework over the years. We still use it today to create real wealth for ourselves and families. Now we have put it together into an easy-to-follow formula in this book.

We lived through the devastation of losing money in the market and getting crushed by taxes.

It was those experiences that led to our mission to change the way Americans save and invest their money, so you can achieve true financial independence with a plan that won't let you down.

America means freedom. It's very different to have financial independence by following a stock market and retirement system designed to enrich those in Wall Street, and a tax system that empowers Washington politicians to take more and more of your money.

Blindly accepting the status quo—the idea that investing in the market using "qualified" plans would create the retirement of my dreams—got me burned.

Even more tragically, the same thing is happening on a huge scale right this minute, to people all across the country.

How to Kill the Status Quo

Does any of this "status quo" conventional wisdom sound familiar?

1. Diversify with mutual funds.
2. Max out 401(k) contributions.
3. Keep your credit score high, and shop for low interest rates.
4. Buy term and invest the difference.
5. Put your money in the market to get a good rate of return.
6. Defer taxes until later. (The reality that exposes this myth is really going to blow your mind.)

All this sounds good, but how many folks are really getting ahead financially following this advice? The problem is we're often taking advice from people who may actually be keeping the truth from us for their own profit.

We've heard the same old tired commentary from experts, gurus and TV personalities for years. Their job isn't to make you wealthy. It's to fill airtime and sell advertising. In short, they are paid to crank out microwave money content as fast as they can to keep their magazines or airtime full.

Likewise, the conventional wisdom preached from the ivory towers of Wall Street was likely never intended to make the average American wealthy. It's engineered for Wall Street's profit.

So, how well has it worked for the average American?

You probably already know the answer because you live it every day. But let's take a look at the proof:

- Half of all households headed by workers aged fifty-five to sixty-four have less than $88,000 in retirement accounts.[1]

- The average American household with at least one credit card has nearly $10,700 in credit card debt.[2]

- Trillions of dollars have evaporated from 401(k) accounts.[3]

- Of those between 45 and 64, 71 percent admit they are worried about having enough money for retirement. [4]

- The average American is paying up to 34.5 percent of their after tax income straight to interest.[5]

- Last year 250,000 new homes went into foreclosure every three months.[6]

In addition to grappling with increasing expenses and debt, the average American has been devastated by losses in investments. Today, the American Association of Retired Persons (AARP) estimates 55 million baby boomers are so concerned about the state of their savings that they are keeping tabs on every penny.

The Jaw Dropping Truth about Wall Street

Who *is* getting rich? The Wall Street firms and their executives, that's who. According to the AFL-CIO in 2009, James Dimon of JP Morgan Chase received $9.2 million in compensation, Goldman Sachs's Lloyd Blankfein received $9.8 in compensation, Wells Fargo's John Stumpf received a jaw dropping $21.3 million and Bank of America's Thomas Montag received a mind blowing $29.9 million for one years' worth of compensation.[7]

Now here's the kicker. These are all banks that received money from the government bailout. The list could go on and on. Go back a few more years to 2005. That year T. Boone Pickens made $1.4 billion. 1.4 *billion* in compensation in *one* year?[8]

Knocks the wind out of you, doesn't it?

Now don't get me wrong, we don't begrudge someone making a fortune for himself. That's what the American Dream is all about. But where does all that money come from to pay those outrageous CEO paychecks?

Is it from manufacturing a product that is sold to a consumer? Is it from building a home, saving a life in a hospital or selling groceries at the store?

Nope.

It's from Wall Street working the system with their super computers to profit regardless of whether the market goes up or down. The computers and brokerage houses use lightning fast algorithms to buy and sell millions of shares a day, executing deals within split seconds. These deals can amount to more than 50 percent of trading volume every day.

Is any real value created by these trades, or is it just a great way to make a lot of money at someone else's expense? These folks create fortunes for themselves, while you, the average citizen, could end up riding the roller coaster of market swings with no control over your money.

But lousy investment returns are just the tip of the iceberg. Another problem is how our money flows—in the front door and out the back without stopping to visit. The average American pays up to 34 percent of his after-tax income in interest charges, saving just a small sliver for himself.[9] If you are like most people who re-finance their mortgage a couple times throughout their lives, you likely aren't paying that low advertised interest rate. You could end up paying as much as 80 percent interest on that mortgage! It's a tried-and-true system set up by bankers to ensure you'll keep paying them interest.

One infamous quote was recorded when someone saw a massive yacht club full of million dollar yachts held exclusively for Wall Street executives. "Where are all the *c-c-customer's* yachts?" he stammered.[10] Good question.

Seems crazy, doesn't it?

It *is* crazy, but that's the status quo.

But that's not you anymore. You're about to discover a whole new world of money. Because *you* are ready to join the ranks of your fellow Americans becoming wealthy outside the Wall Street roller coaster.

There *is* a way to keep a lot more of your money. There *is* a way you can grow wealthy from your hard work—and keep your money protected from market downturns at the same time.

It's easier than you think. The next few chapters are going to show you how to not only kill the status quo but also how to join the ranks of the wealthy.

To get started, just turn the page!

Chapter 2

THE INVISIBLE TAX

"Inflation is when you pay fifteen dollars for the ten-dollar haircut you used to get for five dollars when you had hair."
—Sam Ewing

"Inflation is taxation without legislation"
—Milton Friedman

"By a continuing process of inflation, government can confiscate, secretly and unobserved, an important part of the wealth of their citizens."
—John Maynard Keynes

Through our adventures meeting with millionaire mentors who shared their secrets with us, it became clear that there are four major killers to creating financial independence. We call them the 4 Enemies of Wealth.

These enemies are Taxes, Market Loss, Interest, and Inflation.

We'll deal with each of them in greater detail throughout the rest of this book.

You'll discover why they are "enemies" and what you can do to overcome each of them.

The first one we'll deal with is inflation. Inflation is often misunderstood and often ignored because it's a silent killer of wealth.

You don't write a check to inflation like you do to the IRS, and you don't see money disappear from your retirement account like you do in market crashes.

So, let's look at how inflation happens. Inflation is caused by the government printing money.

A simple way to understand inflation is with an analogy.

Let's say you ask your son Johnny to make Kool-Aid for dinner. He mixes it up just right and it tastes great. But he's *really* thirsty.

So he takes a first drink, and a second, and a few more after that. Now Johnny is in trouble. The Kool-Aid is half gone and he knows he was supposed to save it for dinner . . . but there's no more Kool-Aid mix.

He gets a brilliant idea to fix his problem.

Instead of making more Kool-Aid, he just pours some extra water into the pitcher to fill it back up.

Obviously that's not going to taste good, but he doesn't care because he already had his fill.

The Kool-Aid, in fact, tastes terrible. It's been diluted so the flavor is less potent.

This is essentially what happens when the government prints money. The government is the only entity that can legally print money, and by default, gets to spend it first.

Just like Johnny got to drink the Kool-Aid while it tasted good, the government gets to spend a dollar at its full potency before it's diluted.

After Washington pushes billions of dollars into the money supply, what do you think that does to the value of your money?

It's becomes diluted, just like Johnny's Kool-Aid.

Once it's pushed into the economy, every other dollar in the system becomes less valuable. Your money—and my money—is worth less today than it was yesterday because of the massive and irresponsible money printing going on in Washington.

However, unlike Johnny, who only took a few drinks, the government's thirst for spending is *unquenchable.* Therefore, they continue printing money to the point where our dollar is worth $0.43 compared to 30 years ago. [11]

This is the damage inflation does.

Take a look at this image and see if you remember paying $.99 for a gallon of gas, or $5.00 to go to the movies. Of course you do. It's not that gas is so much more expensive or bread is so much harder to make—it's that our money is worth less now than it was 20 or 30 years ago.

MOVIE TICKET		
1952	1983	2013
$.50	$3.50	$8

LOAF WHITE WONDER BREAD		
1952	1983	2013
$.16	$.51	$2.97

AVERAGE GALLON OF GAS		
1952	1983	2013
$.20	$1.24	$3.58

SNICKERS CANDY BAR		
1952	1983	2013
$.05	$.40	$1.09

McDONALDS HAMBURGER		
1952	1983	2013
$.15	$.50	$3.29

http://www.kgbanswers.com/how-much-did-a-big-mac-cost-in-1983/5022573

This is bad in many ways. The cost of living increases as the price of everyday goods rises faster than wages.

For low- to middle-income Americans, inflation actually pushes people down to a lower standard of living. But it really gets ugly when you look at this in terms of retirement.

Here's why . . .

Let's assume that inflation is at 4% percent. That's a hair higher than what the government typically tells us. But it's hard to know the true inflation rate since the government has changed the way it's calculated multiple times in order to make it look lower than it really is.

(If you calculate inflation with the same measurements the government was using in the 1970s, the inflation rate for the past few years is closer to 5-10%!)[12]

We'll use the Rule of 72 to help us get a feel for the damage inflation is doing to your retirement and wealth.

Albert Einstein is credited with discovering the Rule of 72, and if you aren't familiar with it, it's time to take notes. This is a concept you need to be familiar with and use on a regular basis to help you see the value of growing your money and protecting it from inflation.

The Rule of 72 shows us the amount of time it takes for your money to double, based on a specific interest rate.

If you're getting 4% on your money, 4% divided into 72 gives you 18. That means your money will double every 18 years.

It's a pretty easy calculation to do, and a *very important thing to know.*

The Rule of 72 is a powerful concept because it can work FOR you *or* AGAINST you.

It works *for* when you're growing your money, and *against* you when it's being devalued by inflation.

Using the Rule of 72, take the inflation rate of 4% and divide it into 72, and you get 18 years.

This means the value of your money is being cut in half every 18 years.

For example, in the graphic below, you'll see that if you are age 47 and are comfortable living off $100,000 per year, when you retire at age 65, that same $100,000 will only buy you a $50,000 lifestyle. Your lifestyle will be cut in half unless you have double the money.

Not a pretty picture!

Inflation Cutting Your Money In Half

RATE	YEARS	AGE	ANNUAL INCOME TODAY
4⟌72	18	47	$100,000
			WILL BE LIKE
		65	$50,000

Now, do you plan on living past age 65? I hope so!

Let's say you live another 18 years and last to age 83. That same $100,000 lifestyle you are living today will be more like a $25,000 lifestyle. Are you comfortable with that? I'm not!

RATE	YEARS	AGE	ANNUAL INCOME TODAY
4⟌72	18	47	$100,000
			WILL BE LIKE
		65	$50,000
		83	$25,000

It was SHOCKING to me the first time I saw this.

That's exactly why inflation is such a terrible enemy of wealth, and why we must beat it!

We do that by growing our money with a rate of return that outpaces inflation.

Just a small increase in the rate of return on your money can make a dramatic impact on your wealth, thanks to the power of compound interest.

$$\frac{18}{4\overline{)72}}$$

AGE	4% 18 YEARS
29	$ 10,000
47	$ 20,000
65	$ 40,000

Let's take a newlywed 29-year-old who invests $10,000 at 4% interest. Four divided into 72 is still 18. So his $10,000 is doubling every 18 years and grows to around $40,000 by age 65. Not impressive. Not exciting.

Now he's got a major problem—he's run out of time.

What if instead of getting just 4%, he could have *earned 8%? Would our newly married man now have greater financial independence?*

Of course.

$$\frac{9}{8\overline{)72}}$$

AGE	8% 9 YEARS
29	$ 10,000
38	$ 20,000
47	$ 40,000
56	$ 80,000
65	$ 160,000

At an interest rate of 8%, your money is doubling every 9 years. That's half the time.

Logically, you might think that doubling the interest rate would double your money, so instead of $40,000, you would end up with $80,000.

But you'd be wrong.

With 8% compounded over 36 years, at age 65, you'll actually have around $160,000! You've only increased your return by 4%, but it produced $160,000 vs $40,000. That's four times more money!

That happens because of the power of compound interest.

Now let's see what would happen if you could get 12% on your money and it's doubling every 6 years.

This is where it really gets exciting . . .

$$12\overline{)72} = 6$$

AGE	12% 6 YEARS
29	$ 10,000
35	$ 20,000
41	$ 40,000
47	$ 77,000
53	$ 152,000
59	$ 300,000
65	$ 590,000

In 36 years, at age 65, you've got close to ***$590,000 vs. $40,000.*** *(You probably expected $640,000, but as interest rates get higher, the Rule of 72 becomes a little less accurate.)*

Even so, isn't the difference in amounts amazing?

The only difference between these is the interest rate.

Not more money.

Not more time.

But if you only earn 4%, it just cost you $550,000.

Now you may be asking, how do I grow my money at 8% or 12% in today's market without losing it all when the market tanks?

That's what this book is all about. We'll uncover several strategies we've discovered over the years to outpace inflation and increase your wealth exponentially.

Chapter 3

MY BREAKUP WITH
MR. MARKET

"If I had to give advice, it would be keep out of Wall Street."
— John D. Rockefeller

Ethan Kap wasn't normal.

You could say he had a strange fascination with money. Much more than the average teenager asking for gas money—as a youngster he had a fascination with the idea that by investing his money it could automatically grow year after year. It shouldn't have surprised anyone, then, when he bought his very first mutual fund at the age of *fourteen*. In his words ...

———

It was just a normal day at school—until I overheard a conversation that changed my life. Two parents were talking about how anyone can buy stocks and have their money grow larger and larger each year. Some people even became millionaires in the market! Bursting with excitement, I ran home and told my dad that I wanted to invest in the market. I wanted to make millions! I was delighted when he offered to match my $1,500, and together we researched available funds. With his guidance, I found what I thought was a winner. I invested, watched my money grow over the next five years, and sold at a decent profit.

I was hooked.

Like many people I bounced from one stock to the next, using one strategy after another like a Las Vegas gambler looking for the big win.

I was convinced I'd found my ticket to riches: Warren Buffett. His stock-investment method was simple: He invested in consumer monopolies, or what he called "toll bridges". He did the research, and then bought accordingly. He looked for stocks that were undervalued and held on to them forever—unless the fundamentals of the company changed.

Sounded like a winner to me, so I switched my investing strategy and started buying large blue chip companies like Coca Cola, McDonald's and Colgate. For another five years I did really great.

You can probably guess what happened next.

The stock market crashed.

And because the stock market is no respecter of persons, I—along with everyone else—lost a huge percent of my portfolio in that crash. My dream of watching my dollars multiply had turned into a nightmare.

You may have experienced the sickening, desperate feeling of watching your money evaporate right before your eyes with nothing you can do about it!

My Crushing Break Up with Mr. Market

If you've ever seen a relationship start with a deception or lie, it usually doesn't turn out too well. No matter the initial strength of the romance, the initial deception or lie will cause one party to lose all trust for the other partner.

I lost my trust in Mr. Market when this happened to me. I still have moments where I think about the potential to make money buying and selling stocks again. But I quickly come back to reality when I think about losing another decade of wealth.

Notable Wall Street Crashes and Recoveries [i]

1901-03
- Fall in the Dow: 46%
- Losses recovered by July 1905
- 2 years to recover

1906-07
- Fall in the Dow: 49%
- Losses recovered by September 1916
- 9 years to recover

1916-17
- Fall in the Dow: 40%
- Losses recovered by November 1919
- 2 years to recover

continued on next page

---

continued from previous page

1919-21

- Fall in the Dow: 47%
- Losses recovered by November 1924
- 3 years to recover

1929-32

- Fall in the Dow: 89%
- Losses recovered by November 1954
- 22 years to recover

1939-42

- Fall in the Dow: 40%
- Losses recovered by
- January 1945
- 3 years to recover

1973-74

- Fall in the Dow: 45%
- Losses recovered by December 1982
- 8 years to recover

I realized that continuing to invest directly in the stock market held no guarantees. I had a goal for growing wealthy, and this wasn't helping me reach that goal. All my savings were in the stock market, and I had no control over how that market performed. In fact, there was a very real risk that I could lose *all my money.*

Can You Afford to Lose Another Decade of Wealth?

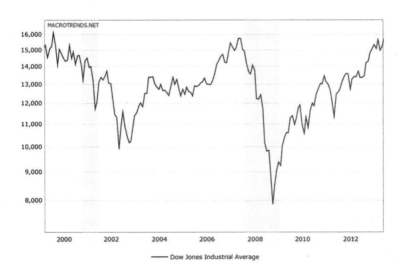

Dow Jones Industrial Average

In September 2013, the Dow Jones Industrial Average was hovering at the same level it was at 14 years before. Trillions of dollars were lost in stocks, mutual funds, 401(k)s and other qualified plans. Mr. Market can be extremely rewarding during certain periods, but viciously brutal during others. Dreams are crushed, retirements dashed and plans delayed. Can you really afford to keep rebuilding your wealth every 5 or 10 years?

The Wall Street Casino

I live close to Vegas and often take trips down with my family. I am always amazed at the luxurious casinos being built. I hear myself saying, "They can't afford to build these huge casinos by paying out winnings to all the customers."

Most people know the house usually wins, yet thousands of people make the trip and continue gambling away their money.

Sadly, many follow the same pattern regarding their wealth: put it at risk in the stock market hoping for that *one* upward swing that will make them extremely wealthy.

I'm sure if someone asked you about taking all their retirement money and gambling it on a roulette wheel; you'd instinctively tell him that's probably not a good idea. Yet that's similar to what people do in the market every day.

It's the difference between the foolish man who built his house upon the sands of risk and the wise man who built his house on a solid financial foundation. The tide came in and destroyed the man's house on the sand. The man's house on the rock survived and remained standing strong.

This is exactly why you must PROTECT the PRINCIPAL at all costs.

Take for example a $100,000 investment. Assume the market drops by 30% and your money goes from $100,000 to $70,000. How much growth do you need just to get back to even? (Hint: it's not 30%.) You'll actually need 42.9% growth on your money to get back to where you started. Now how long does it take to see a 30% loss in the market? It could happen in as little as one year.

And how long does it take to make your money back? Usually it's not so quick. Let's take a look at some examples in history.[13] After the great depression, from 1929-32, the Dow fell 89% and took a full 22 years to recover, Now, 22 years until recovery is a bit dramatic so let's look at a few more recent drops.

In 1973-74, the Dow fell by approximately 45%. The losses weren't recovered until December 1982. That means a full 8 years could have passed without folks getting any return on their money.

And, of course, most recently the crash of 2008. After the market peaked on October 9, 2007, stocks slid downward. By March 5, 2009, the S&P was down 56% and the Dow down 53%. As of this writing, the Dow is still down 3000 points, which is over 21% below where it was 3 years ago. The S&P is still down 24%.

Wall Street seems to have convinced many people that it's necessary to forgo guaranteed returns, and risk principal, in favor of *possible* 8, 10 or even 12% return on their investments.

Wall Street's favorite tool could be considered a financial calculator showing how much money we'll have in retirement if our money grows at 12 or even 15%!

But often those illustrations leave out several major factors like market downturns, taxes and fees.

Unfortunately, due to recent events, we know all too well that even after all the worry, investigation and research, the gains we've had in our retirement—even after years of growth—can be wiped out with a market downturn.

> ### According to the DALBAR Report
>
> "Based on an analysis of actual investor behavior over the 20 years ending December 31, 2007, the average equity investor would have earned an annualized return of 4.4% underperforming the S&P by more than 7% and outpacing inflation by a mere 1.44%." *Quantitative Analysis of Investor Behavior (QAIB)*

In just one year during the great recession of 2008 the Dow Jones Industrial lost 1/3 of its value!

There were more than a few Americans that saw their retirement dreams destroyed right before their eyes as their nest-egg dropped like a rock. They were powerless to do anything about it.

Another flaw in much of this Wall Street conventional wisdom is that the market actually could provide you 12-15% returns in the first place. DALBAR Inc. (the nation's leading financial services market research firm) shows that the average investor outpaced inflation by just 1.44% over the past several years.

But that's not the story we hear coming out of Wall Street. We often hear about great rates of return. People love to talk about a new hot stock or the latest news on a new tech company that could give them a great rate of return. But let's take a closer look.

In our example, Joe starts with $10,000 and gets a 100% rate of return in year one, bouncing his balance up to $20,000.

The next year the market drops by 50% leaving him with $10,000 again. In year three it goes up again by 100% to $20,000. Then drops again in the fourth year by 50%, setting him right back at $10,000.

Year	Market	Starting Balance	Ending Balance
1	+100%	10,000	20,000
2	-50%	20,000	10,000
3	+100%	10,000	20,000
4	-50%	20,000	10,000

In this case the market did average a 25% rate of return. But how much additional cash does Joe have left to show for his 25% average rate of return?

Zero.

Even though brokers quote stats about great rates of return in the market, investors could still be netting absolutely zero.

Take that same $10,000, compound it monthly for four years at 6.5% with no risk in the market, and you could end up with $12,960.20.

A 25% return in the market gave Joe $10,000, but a much lower 6.5% rate, compounded every year, would give him almost $13,000. It's easy to see why people are getting confused about where they should put their money.

> *"In a 2006 report on 401(k) fees, the Government Accountability Office (GAO) concluded that such charges (fees) could "significantly decrease retirement savings."*
>
> Source: Government Accountability Office; www.gao.gov)

Rub Some Salt in the Wound

It's not just market dips that can kill your principal. It's also fees. Often 401(k)s, mutual funds and other stock market related investments come with fees—fees many people don't understand because they can be very confusing.

Compounded over time, this 1-3% fee structure can mean the difference between a comfortable retirement and having to watch every penny. Even if you do realize a 10% return in the market, it could end up being 7-8% after fees.

Even a 1% point difference in fees can have a big impact. Let's take a 35-year-old worker who leaves $20,000 in his 401(k) plan when he switches jobs and never adds to that account. If the Account earned 7% a year, minus 0.5% in annual fees, his balance would only grow to about $139,836 at retirement. But if the fees were 1.5% annually, the average net return would be reduced to 5.5%, and the $20,000 would grow to about $103,747. Over 30 years, the 1% increase in fees whittles down the account balance by over 26%.[14] Even worse, when you tack on fees while you are losing money, it can be very difficult to regain the ground you've lost so you can start making progress again.

You Can't Grow Your Money If It's Shrinking

When I went back to the drawing board for the last time, I didn't listen to what everyone else was doing. I made a list of what *I* needed. I needed a way to save my money and build financial independence that was simple, easy to follow and protected from market crashes—a way that *guaranteed* growth. But that's not all. It also needed to provide good tax benefits because taxes can ravage your wealth if you aren't careful. Oh, and wait—I needed to be able to access my money at any time; without getting clobbered by fees and penalties like you would with 401(k) or IRA qualified plans.

I'm happy to say, I found the perfect solution. It's not a get-rich- quick scheme. But, it's also not gambling with my future. I'm not the only one who's had a bad experience in the market. In fact, many people have been fleeing Wall Street looking for a safer alternative. But many don't know where to look. They are fearful of making a wrong decision and losing even more.

The Wrap

When you start down the *Wealth Beyond Wall Street* path, you'll give yourself permission; permission to toss out the old idea that the only way to become wealthy is to risk your hard earned money. Permission to grow wealthy while protecting against some of the other enemies of wealth.

There is good news. There is a solution. The pathway of the wealthy is simple and proven. Soon you will have a clear plan to replace the conventional wisdom that has failed many people, with a proven solution that can give you relief, hope and faith in your future.

With this book, you will now have the blueprint you need to make the moves that can protect your life, family, and finances by creating a rock on which you can build a financial foundation that you can count on.

Section 2

ACCEPTING A
NEW REALITY

"I must create a system, or be enslaved by another man's."
— William Blake

*"Reasonable people adapt themselves to the world.
Unreasonable people attempt to adapt the world to themselves.
All progress, therefore, depends on unreasonable people."*
— George Bernard Shaw

Chapter 4

MICROWAVE MONEY AND POP CULTURE GURUS

"There are as many opinions as there are experts."
— Franklin D. Roosevelt

"Even when the experts all agree, they may well be mistaken."
— Bertrand Russell

"Bear Stearns is not in trouble!"

"I believe in the Bear Stearns Franchise, at 69 bucks I'm not giving up on the thing!"

These statements were both made by Jim Cramer, of Mad Money CNBC, uttered on March 6th and March 11th, 2008.

11 days later Bear Sterns stock had dropped from $69.00 to $2.00.

Who controls the financial education most people get these days? Think for a second about who most people are listening to. You may have read articles from pop culture money magazines. You might have followed the popular TV personalities or read their books. You may have listened to the HR department at work suggesting you invest in the 401(k) because you'll get matching funds! Free money!

Wait just a minute. Did you know that the 401(k) and other qualified retirement programs are trillion-dollar businesses? By some estimates there are between 7 and 11 trillion dollars in qualified plans. That's a lot of money to trust to Wall Street stockbrokers and their computer systems.

Could it just be possible that there is a little self-interest going on? Might it be that investment bankers, stockbrokers and brokerage houses are *keenly* interested in selling that Wall Street conventional wisdom because that's how they make a living?

Do They Practice What They Preach?

Almost everybody's heard of—if not listened to—Suze Orman, the personal finance expert. Orman hosts her own show, has written a handful of bestsellers and was named by *Time* magazine as one of the world's one hundred most influential people. She encourages viewers, listeners and readers to buy term and invest (remember investing = risking) the difference in mutual funds.

But does she practice what she preaches?

She estimates her liquid net worth at about $25 million, with an additional $7 million in houses. Where is the majority of her money invested?

"I save it and build it in municipal bonds. I buy zero-coupon municipal bonds and all the bonds I buy are triple-A-rated, and insured so even if the city goes under, I get my money." Orman quips.

Doesn't sound like *she's* risking her money in the market does it? That's a wealth beyond Wall Street strategy if I've ever heard one.

When asked about playing the stock market, she says that, "I have a million dollars in the stock market, because if I lose a million dollars, I don't personally care." In short, the financial guru coaching the American public has a portfolio few could live with.

Maybe someone who can afford to lose $1 million has no qualms about encouraging other people to invest in the market, too.

Of course it probably doesn't help that one of her personal sponsors is TD Ameritrade. TD Ameritrade is a huge company who makes money facilitating stock trades. Suze Orman is often seen on advertisements encouraging people to open up an account with TD Ameritrade. Now, does Orman's advice to buy term and invest the difference in the market sound fishy to you?

Then of course there's Jim Cramer, investment guru and host of CNBC's *Mad Money*, who advises that people invest their mad money—or in other words, non-retirement funds—in the stock market. Cramer regularly makes recommendations not only to his own show's viewers but also to audiences of NBC's *Today Show*, steering people to the market buys he thinks will pay off handsomely.

How's that been working?

Not so well, according to news reports. As one example, reported by the *Wall Street Cheat Sheet,* Cramer recommended that viewers buy CIT Group, a stock he said that was primed for upside. Fewer than four weeks later, CIT filed bankruptcy. The *Cheat Sheet's* assessment? "This type of incredibly speculative advice is as radioactive to the general investing public as a post nuclear explosion site... If "In Cramer You Trust", (like the CNBC commercials tell you to do), you are probably going to have lost over 90% of your investment by the open on Monday."[15]

Summing it all up, a report in *Baron's* stated that, "Cramer is wildly inconsistent, and the performance of individual picks varies widely. So widely, in fact, that it is impossible to know with confidence that any sample of Cramer's recommendations will enable you to outperform the market."[16]

These are just two examples of the media promoting the Wall Street conventional wisdom—that has a questionable (at best) track record of success, and often proves just the opposite! In fact, they've done such a good job convincing Americans of the conventional financial wisdom of investing in stock, maxing out 401(k)s, buying term and then investing the difference, that we've seen millions of people lose trillions of dollars by following each other like sheep right off the financial cliff.[17]

Those who grow wealthy outside the stock market roller coaster are building their house on a solid foundation. Contractors don't put buildings on foundations of clay or sand. They use concrete. Why then would we be any less careful with our entire financial future? The solid foundation we are talking about is safer places to save money. It's the safety net you can count on in good times and bad. People who have their money outside of Wall Street don't worry about the market roller coaster. They have their foundation growing without risk, plus, they give themselves many other living benefits. We'll get to those shortly.

The Wrap

So far on our Wealth Beyond Wall Street path, we've covered three critical topics:

1. Wall Street conventional financial wisdom has failed many Americans. It's time to leave the status quo behind.

2. Investing in the market holds no guarantees. It is more like building your financial house on a foundation of sand.

3. Pop culture financial gurus get paid to fill airtime, not make you wealthy. In fact following their advice can cost you big time.

But the fun doesn't end there. There's another force we have to contend with. An extraordinary story about a bank robber named Willie Sutton might shed some light on it for you.

Chapter 5

THE WILLIE SUTTON SLAP DOWN

"In this world nothing can be said to be certain, except death and taxes."

—Benjamin Franklin

Willie Sutton wasn't born a bank robber.

Willie was the fourth of five children born to an ordinary Brooklyn family on June 30, 1901. Like all the other kids in Brooklyn, he went to school. But he didn't stick with it very long. Filled with dreams, he left home after the eighth grade in search of fame and fortune.

But Willie had a problem. He loved expensive clothes and the finer things of life—things that were hard to finance on the meager wages he brought in from his string of menial jobs like gardening, clerking and drilling. Never satisfied, he jumped from one job to another with alarming frequency. His longest period of continuous employment was 18 months.

At the age of 28, he got married. But his wedded bliss was short-lived because his wife divorced him when he landed in jail. You see, Willie Sutton had finally found a career that offered fatter paychecks, albeit riskier working conditions. Willie Sutton was a bank robber.

After serving a brief stint, Willie was back on the streets and back at his lucrative profession. According to the FBI, Willie Sutton mastered the art of disguise—a talent that earned him the nickname, "The Actor". He attempted to rob the Corn Exchange Bank and Trust Company in Philadelphia, Pennsylvania disguised as a mailman. The curiosity of a passerby derailed his plans. (Not to worry: he returned to the same bank less than a year later and this time was successful.) At other times, he disguised himself as a messenger, policeman or maintenance man. He pulled off a sizable heist at a Broadway jewelry store in broad daylight by disguising himself as a telegraph messenger.

In addition to his innovative disguises, Willie was distinguished from other bank robbers by his gentle demeanor. Victims of his robberies and innocent bystanders in the teller lines reported how polite he was. Many commented that he behaved like a real gentleman. One victim quipped that witnessing a Willie Sutton robbery was like being at the movies, except the usher had a gun.

In June 1931, Willie's luck ran out—sort of. He was charged with assault and robbery, found guilty, and sentenced to 30 years in prison. But again that 18-month charm kicked in. 18 months after he was incarcerated, just in time to celebrate Christmas in 1932, Willie roped two nine-foot sections of ladder together and scaled up and over the prison wall.

On February 5, 1934, Willie returned to the Corn Exchange Bank and Trust Company—this time with a machine gun. Things didn't go so well. He was apprehended and sentenced to serve 25 to 50 years in the Eastern State Penitentiary in Philadelphia.

Fast-forward to April 3, 1945. Willie Sutton was one of 12 convicts who burrowed out of the penitentiary through a tunnel—his *fifth* escape attempt from the same prison. Philadelphia police officers recaptured him the same day. He was tossed back in prison, this time for life as a fourth-time offender. Just to be on the safe side, officials transferred him to the Philadelphia County Prison in Holmesburg, Pennsylvania—away from the prison where he'd practiced so many escapes.

Willie lasted almost two years at Holmesburg before he and a group of other prisoners dressed up as prison guards, sashayed across the prison yard after dark and carried two ladders to the prison wall. Caught in the beams of the prison searchlight, Willie Sutton flashed a grin and yelled, "It's okay," and kept moving with his plan. No one stopped him. He was free again.

On March 20, 1950, a little more than three years after he walked away from Holmesburg, Willie Sutton was added to the FBI list of Ten Most Wanted Fugitives. In addition to distributing his poster to police departments throughout the nation, the FBI also gave his photograph to tailors. After all, this was a man who dressed impeccably in expensive, tailored clothing. Two years later, Willie was nonchalantly riding a New York City subway when a twenty-four-year-old tailor's son recognized him as the man from the wanted posters. He quietly followed Willie to a gas station and watched him buy a battery for his car before he called the police with the tip.

Face-to-face with New York's finest, Willie didn't resist arrest. But he also didn't fess up to any robberies—or any other crimes, for that matter. He was hauled into Queens County Court, where he was sentenced to an additional 30 years to life. It was a drop in the bucket. Willie already owed one life sentence plus 105 years. They tossed him into a cell at Attica State Prison and threw away the key. If all went according to plan, he'd never see daylight again.

Of course, that wasn't the end of the story. Seventeen years later, the system took pity on Willie. He was seriously ill with emphysema and needed major surgery on the arteries in both his legs. On Christmas Eve of 1969, the State of New York released Willie Sutton from prison. He was sixty-eight. Just two years later in an irony that's stranger than fiction, Willie did a television commercial to promote the new photo credit card for—what else?—a Connecticut bank.

Willie Sutton died November 2, 1980 at the age of 79. Before he died, he authored two books about his illustrious career as a bank robber. When asked why he robbed banks, he smiled and replied, "Because that's where the money is." [18]

Willie Sutton's Law

Why did Willie rob banks? Willie said it best himself: he robbed banks because that's where the money was. Wherever wealth is accumulated, someone will always try to take it. In some circles, this type of human behavior is called, "Willie Sutton's Law".

If you are like most Americans, you may feel you are living Willie Sutton's Law every day. Shallow bank balances, high expenses, credit card statements and bills on the counter make us feel as though someone is constantly trying to take our money away!

But before you sell the car, cut up the credit cards and stop buying food for the dog, let's take a better look at exactly who might be trying to rob you. The following tactics are completely legal, and unless you are aware, you might not even see them coming.

Who is the modern day Willie Sutton imposter? It is the Tax Man.

But, wait! Shouldn't we all share the cost of doing business in this country, by sharing the costs of education, paving roads and running the government? Sure—that was the idea. But if you're not careful, and if you blindly follow the Wall Street conventional wisdom by investing in qualified retirement plans, you may one day have a sickening scene unfold in front of you. You could end up losing a massive chunk of your retirement to taxes, much more than you bargained for. There's a legal and ethical way to prevent that, and you'll be excited when you see how simple it is to accomplish.

Under the Tax Man's Thumb

You are probably aware that, depending on your tax bracket, the Tax Man could be grabbing up to 20-30% of your paycheck every pay period. (Did you know that Thomas Jefferson said that an income tax of even 1% is equivalent to slavery?) Wait a minute. Wasn't it you that commuted in rush hour traffic, dealt with upset customers and missed out on the kids' baseball games while working those 50+ hour weeks? You do the all work, yet the Tax Man always takes his cut.

But income tax is just the beginning—the proverbial tip of the iceberg. Take a second and think of all the other taxes you might be paying: state income tax, social security tax, property tax, Medicare tax, phone tax, utility tax, sales tax, gasoline tax and vehicle tax—not just on the purchase, but also on the annual registration. And in the next few years, we could be looking at unprecedented levels of healthcare taxes.[19] In fact, almost every transaction you make is taxed.

Consider your average morning. Almost every time you brush your teeth, turn on a light, eat a bowl of cereal, use the phone or access the Internet, taxes take a bite.

When you get in your car, drive down the road, go out to lunch, or even take out the trash, the Tax Man is right there in the shadows, like Willie Sutton, to take your money. It's enough to drive you crazy. So doesn't it seem sheer lunacy, then, to pay even more taxes on the money you save for retirement?

The Trillion Dollar Tax Target

Hey, wait a minute! Hasn't the government established tax-deferred programs to help people save and invest for retirement *without* paying taxes up front? Indeed, but remember Willie Sutton's Law? Wherever wealth is accumulated, someone will be there to steal it.

Do you have any idea how much wealth is accumulated in government-sponsored qualified retirement plans like IRAs and 401(k)s?

Trillions of dollars

If you aren't careful, the profits of these plans could end up largely being Uncle Sam's. Here's why. Imagine for just a minute that you're a farmer. You purchase a bag of corn seed. As the sun begins to dip below the horizon on that late spring evening, you gaze out over your fields, filled with the anticipation of an abundant harvest following months of sustained labor.

As time goes by, you do everything right. You fertilize, water, weed, tend and protect. At last comes the time of harvest and the abundance you imagined is realized ten times over. You're filled with the satisfaction of a job well done as you watch a convoy of trucks taking your crops to market.

As the last trailer disappears from sight, a shiny sedan roars up, tires crunching in the gravel at the edge of the road. Out hops a well-dressed man who looks suspiciously like Willie Sutton. As you remove your hat and wipe your well-worn sleeve across your dampened brow, he opens a notebook and stands with ballpoint pen ready. Without so much as an introduction—because, really, he doesn't need one—he poses the question: So, farmer, you have two options. Do you want to pay taxes on that bag of seed you hauled in here last spring or on the five trucks of crops you just sent to market?

He's kidding, right?

No. He's not. Let's pretend you, the farmer, had a choice: you can pay taxes on the seed—the money you start out with—or you can pay taxes on the crop, which represents all the increase that grew from your initial seed money.

In the government-sponsored, tax-deferred retirement plans, you pay taxes on all the increase. You're paying taxes on the truckloads of crops. With the approach we'll show you, you pay taxes on the seed. The crops are yours, and you get to keep all the money you grow.

To help you more clearly understand how this works, let's look at some actual figures.

Option 1: A post-tax plan like a Roth IRA

Invest $5,000 a year for 30 years.

Total of $150,000.

In a 33% tax bracket you pay $49,500 in taxes on that money as you earn it over the 30 years.

Assume you experience a 6.5% growth rate on that money. By the end of the 30 years, you'll have $333,903.28 in your account.

Option 2: A tax-deferred plan like a 401(k)

Invest $5,000 a year in the stock market for 30 years.

Growth rate: 6.5%

Total of $498,363.11.

You didn't pay taxes up front on this money, so you've now got more money. Okay, you're probably thinking, this is a no-brainer—I'll take the tax-deferred plan with the bigger balance!

But wait: remember Willie Sutton? He's clicking his ballpoint pen. How much of that $498,363.11 belongs to Uncle Sam? You have $498,363.11 in your retirement account. Let's say you take out $73,000 a year to live on during retirement. You can take $73,000 a year out of your account for nine years before your money is gone (assuming it's still growing at 6.5%). On that $73,000 each year, you now have to pay taxes on the "crop" (assuming you are in the same 33% tax bracket). Thus, you will pay $24,090 in taxes every year. In nine years, you will have paid $216,810 in taxes.

Remember how much you saved by deferring taxes—by waiting to pay on the crop instead of on the seed? You saved $49,500. That means you will have paid Uncle Sam back everything you saved in just the first two and a half years. In the next six and a half years, you will pay an additional $167,310 in taxes on your harvest.

In fact, according to Scott Shultz, you could end up paying up to five times more taxes using a qualified plan like a 401(k), than you saved during your entire working years.[20]

Now ask yourself that question again: Would I rather pay taxes on my seed or on my crop?

Conventional wisdom says you'll be in a lower tax bracket when you retire, so deferring taxes is a good thing. Not so fast. In later years, people often lose many of the deductions they presently have because kids have moved out and mortgages have been paid off.

Plus, do you know what the tax rates are going to be when you retire? How does the Federal Government plan to pay back the trillion-dollar deficit? None of us, not even the most seasoned prognosticator, can predict where taxes will be when you retire. But a quick look back into history shows tax brackets that have been as high as 92%.

The good news is that you don't have to pay on your crop. We'll show you how to beat old Willie Sutton by paying on your seed so you can enjoy your full harvest. By paying on your seed, you are still meeting your tax obligation. This difference is, you're just not over-paying.

Paying tax on the seed gives you major tax advantages on your growth, while at the same time protecting the principal from risks in the market. You also can have access to your money throughout your life (even if that's next month or next year or all the way into your retirement). It also allows you to transfer your wealth to your heirs without them having to pay income tax on that money.

The Wrap

The Wealth Beyond Wall Street path is not just about keeping your money protected from market losses. It's about shielding your money from all the enemies of wealth, like taxes, market losses and brokerage fees.

But it doesn't end there. It gives you another arrow in your arsenal to defeat another foe: the interest vampire.

Chapter 6

KILLING THE INTEREST VAMPIRE

"There are two types of people in the world.
Those who pay interest and those who EARN it."

—Unknown

"The rich rule over the poor, and
the borrower is servant to the lender."

—Proverbs 22:7

"Banks don't lend their money.
They lend the money somebody else left there."

—Adam Smith

I was shocked when I awoke from my zombie-like state.

Much like you, my day was pretty routine. I woke up, went to work, came home, saw the family, ate dinner, went to sleep and did it all over again the next morning, Every two weeks the paycheck came in and immediately disappeared going to mortgage payments, car payments, credit card payments and other expenses.

At the end of the month, I had worked hard. But had little to show for it. I was a member of the financial living dead. Going through the motions to pay everyone else, but not myself.

Like most Americans, I was having the financial life sucked right out of me by the vampire of interest.

How would you like a 34% raise? Of course you would.

If you're an average American, you could be paying a whopping 34% of your after-tax income in interest.[21]

Take out a twenty from your wallet, rip a 1/3 of it off, and that's about how much of your after-tax income could be going to interest every year.

You might be saying to yourself, I shop really hard for good interest rates. I check not only the price of what I'm buying, but I also work hard to keep my credit score high so I can get a good interest rate on my purchases.

Price and *interest rate* are the two factors everyone focuses on—but they're not the things that kill you. The killer is the *volume* of interest

Imagine you go buy a car for $30,000 and get a five-year loan with an interest rate of 7.5%. How much will you pay in interest over the life of that loan? Easy, you say, whipping out your calculator: 7.5% of $30,000 is $2,250.

Wise Money Alert

Your 7.5% car loan could end up costing you more like 20.2% by the time you pay off that loan!

Right?

Wrong! You'll actually pay more than twice that much. The amount of interest you will pay on that $30,000 car loan could be up to $6,068.31—20.2% of the amount you borrowed.

Wait! How is that possible?

It happens because of three letters that follow your interest rate quote: APR, or annual percentage rate. The 7.5% is the rate you pay on the balance of the loan every year. So by the time you are done paying off your car loan, you'll have paid over 20% on that loan, not just 7.5%!

Here's where the volume of interest comes in. Let's say, over the course of your lifetime, you finance 10 cars at $30,000 each. That's a total of $300,000. Assuming you get the same 7.5% interest on those loans, that means you'll pay about $6,000 in interest on each loan, or $60,000 in interest on your 10 cars. I don't know about you, but I think $60,000 is a big deal. A really big deal—especially when current figures reveal that the average American reaches retirement age with

> **Wise Money Alert**
>
> If you thought interest on cars was hard to swallow, this might really make you sick.
>
> Home loans are front loaded with most of the interest paid in the first years of the loan.
>
> Because of how often people refinance homes, over 10 or 20 years of paying down mortgages, up to 86% of every dollar you pay on your mortgage could be going straight to interest!

only $88,000 in savings. That means you will have dumped out, in interest on cars, almost as much as most people save for their entire retirement. (We won't even cover leasing here. Leasing cars can often turn out to be even worse than traditional financing.)

With purchase price and interest combined on your 10 cars, even if you keep them until they're paid off, you will have kissed away $360,000 on your cars. We're talking a total of *four times* what many people save for their retirement.

What if you could keep the majority of that $360,000 flowing back into YOUR pocket instead of some lender or car company?

You can.

I'll introduce you to this great financial tool, and multiple others. Let's get started.

Section 3

BUILDING ON A STRONG FOUNDATION

"Do you wish to rise? Begin by descending. You plan a tower that will pierce the clouds? Lay first the foundation."

— Saint Augustine

Chapter 7

DEFEATING THE
ENEMIES OF WEALTH

*"Wherever wealth is accumulated someone
will be there to try and steal it."*

—R. Nelson Nash

Jason Smith slid into the front seat, slammed the door and slumped forward until his forehead pressed against the steering wheel. His stomach was in knots and a dull ache throbbed behind his temples. Another roller coaster week in the market had dropped his 401(k) value substantially.

He dreaded facing Susan. After all, it had been *his* idea to max out the 401(k). She'd wanted to keep their contributions smaller—to put some of Jason's salary in a conventional savings account or maybe some short-term CDs. She worried about emergencies and about covering the kids' college expenses—all arguments that he disregarded at the time.

He'd read some articles written by the industry's top gurus—
and he figured he knew what he was doing. He knew that the
401(k) was the most popular retirement plan in America. He
not only wanted all the free money he could get through his
employer's match, but he'd heard about the great tax savings to
be had from socking the maximum amount possible into a 401(k).
All the other guys in his department were doing it and they seemed
savvy enough.

Jason had won out, and for the past six years a large percentage
of every paycheck had gone to his 401(k) account. It had seemed
like a good idea at the time. But that was *before.*

Before the market experienced a nearly unprecedented crash
that slashed the value of mutual funds and crushed retirement
accounts of people all over the country.

Before he'd found out—how had he not known this?—that the
money in his 401(k) might as well have been locked up in Fort
Knox, because it was a major pain to get at any of it.

After all, it was *his* money. And he needed some of it.

And now—easing reluctantly up the driveway—Jason knew
that what had seemed like such a good idea six years ago was
turning out to be an emotional and financial rollercoaster with
more downs than ups.

Jason sunk into the sofa in the living room and proceeded
to tell Susan the bad news. Another drop in economic forecasts
had caused a major drop in the market, which was costing them
thousands with every time drop. First off, his account was not
even worth *half* of what he thought it was. His hard-earned money

was gone, thanks to the plunge of a market over which he had no control. So much for his plan of retiring with millions like he'd dreamed about.

Second, Susan had really wanted to access some money for the kitchen remodel they badly needed. If he took the money out, he'd be slapped with so many fees and penalties—including an enormous tax penalty—that he'd scarcely even break even.

Even if he decided to brave the penalties, he'd lose a fortune selling the funds in his account when the market was so low. He would kiss away what hadn't already been lost to the market crash.

Finally, he didn't even dare borrow from his account. That little carrot that had been dangled in front of his nose six years ago turned out to have a very painful string attached. What they hadn't told Jason when he invested in a 401(k) was that if he lost his job, the loan would be due in full, usually within two months' time.

With a rumored corporate merger in the works that could result in potential layoffs that was a chance Jason couldn't afford to take.

Maxing out the 401(k)—not the best idea, Jason sheepishly admitted.

A few days later, after a few emails between friends, Jason got a link to an online site with a 27 second retirement quiz. He was intrigued.

It would tell him how long his retirement savings would last. He started punching in numbers, thinking things couldn't possibly get worse, and while he was a bit shocked at what he saw, he also got some good news.

The bad news; Jason Smith would run out of money at age 71.

Simply put, based on his current plan and the income he felt he would need during retirement he would only have enough income till he reached age 71.

Seventy-one? Jason wondered, what would he do then!

As visions of greeting customers at the local warehouse store clouded his thoughts, he noticed the website offered a way out and it could all be explained by a Wealth Beyond Wall Street™ professional. Let's just say it was a hard sell for Susan. We can imagine why she might be just a little skeptical about Jason's financial know-how right about now.

Reluctantly, Susan agreed, and Jason called to schedule an appointment with a Wealth Beyond Wall Street professional. They had a short 20 minute conversation with Michael. At the end of the conversation he offered them a customized blueprint to help them grow their money safely outside the stock market with major tax advantages. He offered to show them how the entire process works in black and white right from their own computer. Michael is one of the few professionals specifically trained to implement these solutions, so he uses the phone and internet to help people all across the country.

It was done using a 100-year-old proven strategy for keeping money growing outside the Wall Street roller coaster. It came with the potential for double digit growth if the markets went up and with complete downside protection. It could also give you the ability to access your cash value throughout your life. In fact, that was one of the major benefits—that you could use it to Finance Yourself to Wealth™. This meant you could borrow against your cash value for major purchases like cars, college tuition or vacations and then pay your loan back to yourself while the cash continued to grow as if you hadn't touched it. Jason was particularly intrigued by that idea. Ultimately, it was a way to possibly reduce the amount of interest he would pay to banks or credit card companies!

Let's take a break in the story while we're waiting for Michael to call and get a few of the basics out of the way. Because whether you have a 401(k) or not, this will be new information. And like GI Joe says, "Knowing is half the battle".

You might have assumed, just like our friend Jason, that a 401(k) or mutual fund was a solid way to save for retirement. After all, that's what many of the pop culture gurus advocate. Right out of the gate, let's see what one financial analyst had to say about it:

> *The American public has been hoodwinked by political and corporate forces into relying on the 401(k) as the primary long-term investment mechanism. In doing so, the stock market has been put at center stage in providing for a comfortable retirement for the average American. The 401(k) represents an implicit promise to middle-class Americans that they can live off the income that they receive from stock ownership, just like the rich do. It is a promise impossible to fulfill; it is the great 401(k) hoax.*[22]

Hoax sounds like a pretty strong word, but that's potentially what the 401(k) plan is.

Here's a quick crash course on 401(k) plans. Money in 401(k) plans is often invested in stocks and mutual funds. If the market goes up, so can your money. If you have money in a 401 (k) with stocks or mutual funds, your money could be at risk for loss!

That means if the market goes down, you can lose. Lastly, your 401(k) contributions are made *before* you pay taxes on the money, so you're taxed as you withdraw money from the plan. (Here's where you see that you are being taxed on the crop, not the seed.) And don't forget, your money could be tied up until you retire, unless you want to pay the penalties and taxes on an early withdrawal.

Now, let's get back to the meeting with Michael.

━━━━━━━

It's five o' clock on Thursday evening, and Jason and Susan are sitting in front of the computer when Michael calls. Jason is all ears. But Susan, feeling like she's just had the proverbial blanket yanked out from under her feet with the 401(k) debacle, is hanging back. Susan, still skeptical, and goes for the jugular with this comment:

"I need to ask something, right up front," she says. Michael welcomes the question. After detailing what had just happened with their 401(k), Susan squares herself up in her chair. "We've listened to other financial gurus and advisors and it's gotten us where we are now. Why should we listen to you?" she asks.

"I understand your skepticism in talking with another financial professional. The difference is, I'm focused on safer strategies. I help people build a strong foundation of safety so my clients never lose money in market downturns. 401(k) plans or mutual funds can be the *risky* kind of investing," Michael explains. "In fact, depending on how you direct your contributions, it could put your entire retirement principal at risk." Susan, clearly frustrated, glares at Jason.

"Tonight I'm going to talk to you about some of the biggest enemies of building wealth and also about how you can start on the path to becoming a wealthy outside Wall Street.

A couple of the threats that we must protect against to build wealth are, 1) the actual loss of your money in the market (once you lose money, it can take a substantial amount of time to make it up), 2) taxes, and 3) interest. Many folks don't know it, but they could be paying up to one-third of every dollar they make towards interest of some sort. This is essentially making them employees of the tax man and the lenders at the same time."

"Let's talk about putting your money at risk of loss. To begin, let's look at how your mutual fund or stock performs. How much money you end up with for retirement usually depends completely on the market," Michael explains. "The market is uncertain, risky and completely out of your control. So your future is tied to how well the market cooperates, without any input from you."

While Jason and Susan tried to wrap their heads around that piece of information, Michael started asking some pretty tough questions. "Jason, how much do you really know about your 401(k)?"

"Clearly not as much as I thought I did," Jason mumbles.

"Well, let's start with your 401(k) manager—do you even know who it is?" Jason shakes his head, and Michael goes on. "Do you know what funds you're invested in or even what companies your funds invest in? Most people enrolled in 401(k) plans can't even list the funds or companies in which they are investing. That's risky business."

"Interesting," Susan smugly replies. "That sounds more like *gambling* to me."

"There's more," Michael says. "I know that you've already found out about some of the tax implications. Think about this: if you don't like paying taxes right now, what makes you think you're going to like it any better 20 years from now? When you start to withdraw your 401(k) money for retirement, you're going to have to pay taxes on it. That means if you're in a 28% tax bracket, you could have about one-third less actual money than you have in your account."

(A quick tip: in a 401(k) plan, you'll be paying taxes on the crop, not the seed. And this is called tax savings? What an irony. People invest in a 401(k) plan to save taxes, but in reality, they could end up actually paying *more* taxes—not only because they're paying on the crop, but because they could potentially be in a higher tax bracket when they begin taking distributions from their 401(k) plans.)

"You've got three children, right?" Michael asks. Susan says, "yes." "If you don't manage to use up your 401(k) during your retirement, it will be passed on to your heirs. Not only could they face income tax on the money they receive from your 401(k), but they could have to pay estate taxes as well. If you have more than $1 million in your estate, it could amount to 55%.

There's another issue with a 401(k) plan you need to be aware of—fees. Many folks don't know how much in fees they are really paying. Unfortunately, it can add up to a substantial sum, and the fund managers always get paid whether your money grows or not."

Jason slaps his palm against the table. "I feel like I've been misled!" he cries. "Our HR guy pushed a bunch of papers in front of me and encouraged me to sign on the dotted line, all the while touting matching funds and company support. But he never said anything about getting out! All the gurus on TV, and everyone else for that matter, say to max out my 401(k).

Susan clears her throat loudly. "Oh, yeah, well—everyone except Susan," Jason admits.

Now, both Jason and Susan are now ready to listen to Michael. He's shown them why the old way wasn't working. Jason feels like he's learned more about the 401(k) program in the last 20 minutes than in the previous two decades.

Susan, who has softened a little toward Jason says, "I'm feeling ripped off, too. Just yesterday, I read a column by a well-respected financial guru. Her advice was to buy term and invest the difference in mutual funds. It's ironic that she was the spokesperson for TD Ameritrade who probably makes millions of people who invest in the market through their system!"

Jason chuckles. "Yeah, we've both seen the results of those."

How efficient do you think the average business would be if it suffered constant turnover—in other words, if new people came in on a regular basis, bringing new ideas and new ways of doing things? Well, that's what happens with mutual funds—except instead of people, the turnover involves stocks (in other words, excessive trading in the portfolio). Mutual fund managers are constantly changing the stocks in the portfolio. (Translation: you never know from one day to the next exactly *what's* in your portfolio.)

continued on the next page

continued from previous page

In the 1950s, the average portfolio turnover rate was about 15%. Today, 100% turnover is commonplace, and as much as 300% turnover is typical. Just a few years ago, *Forbes* magazine reported turnover rates so high that even the reporter was astonished. Rates ranged from 523% to a staggering 827%. The result of all these turnovers is that the cost of doing business for mutual funds, instead of going down, has doubled since the 1950s. And who pays for the increased cost? That's right: the investors. Lucky dogs.[23]

"We all watched as the market toppled," says Michael, "taking with it the retirement dreams of millions of Americans. Even those who had enjoyed growth watched as their nest eggs were crushed to nearly half their previous value. And they were powerless to do anything about it. But, you know what?" Michael continues, "Even without the disastrous crash we recently witnessed, there are always ups and downs that we can't control. Studies have shown that over the past 180 years that the average market return after factoring for inflation is as low as 1.2%.[24]

"Here's what it amounts to," Michael says. "As an investor, you put up 100% of the money, and you take 100% of the risk. *You're* the one whose principal is on the line. This is fine if you have money you can stand to lose, but this is NOT the way that that savvy investors live. They build a solid foundation and protect the principal. You guys got started on the right foot by visiting our site www.wealthbeyondwallstreet.com right?"

"Yeah, I found your site because a friend referred it to me. I took the Wealth Beyond Wall Street Quiz*, and it was really eye opening. I felt like it was time to try a different approach."

Susan interjects, "The Wealth Beyond Wall Street program sounds good to me."

"It does make sense," Jason agrees. "But I'm not sure what to do at this point. I'm stuck in a crummy 401(k) I can't get out of, and I'm not thinking I can afford any mutual funds for a while— at least not until we pull out of the hole we're in. So, what do we do now?"

Michaels laughs and says to Jason, "Jason, I've got great news for you."

"It's about time I got some *good* news for a change!" Jason laughs.

"You're a whole lot better informed now than before our meeting," Michael points out. "And now I'm going to show you how you *can* get on the right track, starting today. Regardless of your situation with the 401(k) I think we'll find some good solutions together. "I'm going to show you multiple strategies that will keep your money safely out of the market, and offer smart strategies that allow you to Finance Yourself to Wealth™ and can also provide good rates of return. You could reduce or totally eliminate the amount you pay in interest to banks and credit card companies, plus, have access to your cash value throughout your life. Plus, they are strategies you can start right away. Sound good?"

Jason looks like he's about to cry again—this time from relief.

*www.wealthbeyondwallstreet.com/quiz

Chapter 8

THE 6 WEALTH BEYOND WALL STREET STRATEGIES

"All truths are easy to understand once they are discovered; the point is to discover them."

—Galileo

Michael smiled. "There are some options I really like for an incredibly effective portfolio. You may not have heard of most of them. Let's start with silver."

Precious Metals

This surprised Jason. "Silver? I thought gold was all the rage."

"Silver's not the most popular investment, but it's powerful for a couple of important reasons. First, you can start small. You can buy silver for twenty to fifty bucks for a one-ounce coin, depending on the market."

"And I imagine that fluctuates."

"Yes, and that is one of the negatives of silver. It's not going to spin off passive income, and it's at the mercy of what the market says it's worth. But it's never worth zero. That's a major benefit—when inflation is going up the way it is now, silver holds its value. Investing in precious metals can help you hedge against inflation.

"In addition, it's liquid—meaning you can almost always use it to purchase something or get U.S. dollars for it immediately, if needed. So it's great to have in emergencies."

"So tell me why you prefer silver to gold. Or do you suggest purchasing gold as well?"

"I prefer silver because it's a lot easier for most people to get started with than gold. Today, you can buy an ounce of gold for $1300, or you can buy an ounce of silver for $20.

"On the downside, silver is more volatile than gold, so the price moves around a bit more. We're not going to depend on silver for our entire retirement. I recommend having somewhere around 10% of your portfolio in silver and gold as a 'safety net,' not a retirement plan. However, it's an asset that can protect us from several of the enemies of wealth."

Market-Linked CDs

"Next is a strategy called 'market-linked CDs'. A CD is a Certificate of Deposit. It's a financial product you can put your money into, and has two things going for it. It's secure—it's FDIC insured, just like a bank account—and it gives you a little better rate of return than a savings account, although not much.

"The cons are twofold. A CD does lock your money away for a couple of years, so it's not really very liquid, although you can often get loans by using it as collateral, if needed. Plus, the return can be pretty meager when it comes to combating inflation.

But we're talking about something most people have never heard of before. It's an interesting variation to the traditional CD.

"The exciting thing about the *'market-linked'* CD is that you could actually get a higher rate of return than a traditional CD because it's linked to stock market performance.

"What's interesting is that this strategy was developed by big banks and Wall Street firms about 30 years ago specifically for their ultra-rich clients. These clients demanded a better return on their money, but still wanted it to be protected. So for years, the ultra-rich have had access to a tool that most average Americans have no idea is even available!"

"I'm not a risk taker, remember? The stock market makes me a little nervous."

"That's what's neat about this special type of market-linked CD," Michael explained. "You aren't actually risking your money in the market. Your principal is still totally protected and guaranteed, but you get a little more potential growth if the market goes up because your growth is linked to the market."

"Who guarantees it?"

"It's backed by a fully insured FDIC bank— they've just been a bit more creative about how to structure them to allow for a higher rate of return. We'll talk a bit more about the idea of getting the ups of the market with no downside risk. The growth can be much higher than with a typical CD rate."

"Okay, that sounds less frightening. I might even be getting a little bit excited."

"Yeah, just wait until I show you the next couple of options—they'll get you really excited. Keep in mind that most banks don't offer these to their average customers, but I have access to several that do, so if you're interested in that route, I can point you in the right direction."

Annuities

"Another strategy that can create safety with a decent return on your money is something called an indexed annuity, and it's a very popular and protected retirement strategy.

"Twenty years ago, annuities got a bad rap from financial advisors selling them to seniors who didn't know what they were getting. Once the seniors passed away, their families would end up losing a large portion of their money. The seniors, of course, never intended for that to happen, but this created major problems.

"Those days are gone. The annuity companies have made significant changes to their products to ensure that doesn't happen anymore. Now there's usually a death benefit associated with the annuity so if the owner dies, the family can get paid back the entire amount.

"Also, other negatives you may hear about annuities are in reference to the risk and cost of variable annuities.

"One of the most popular annuities today is called a Fixed Indexed Annuity. These are different from variable annuities which expose your money to market losses, because you are basically buying stocks or mutual funds inside an insurance wrapper.

"The variable annuity fee structure is much like mutual funds because they can include up-front sales charges and ongoing administrative and money management fees as a percentage of your cash account value as well. This can get very expensive.

"Fixed Indexed Annuities offer 5 major benefits. First, you get 100% principal protection.* Second, you get a guaranteed rate of return that is locked in every year. This is why it's called 'fixed.'

"Third, they can be bought using qualified money from a 401(k) or IRA, without penalty and without tax consequences. You simply roll money from one qualified account to another.

"Fourth, they can also offer a guaranteed income for life. This is truly a powerful tool because your income is guaranteed by the insurance company, so it's never at risk in the market . . . and you can literally have an income that's guaranteed for life."

"And where does the indexing come in?"

"That's the fifth benefit. The fixed indexed annuity can grow your money when the market goes up but your money is still protected during down markets. This is called 'indexing' and I'll explain how this works in just a minute. Keep in mind there is a limit on this growth called a 'cap.' The powerful thing here is that your growth is locked in each year, so you never have to worry about losing your principal."

"Another benefit is that the fees in a fixed indexed annuity are very low. In most cases you aren't charged an ongoing fee as a percentage of your cash account value like you would pay on a mutual fund. And often companies will even offer a bonus of 5%-10% during the first year.

*   Guarantees backed by the claims paying ability of the underwriting insurance company.

"This means if you bought a $100,000 annuity with a 5% bonus, the insurance company would credit your cash account value $5000 and you would start with $105,000."

"Keep in mind you only want to look at an annuity as a medium to long term strategy. They almost all have surrender charges that are assessed if you withdraw funds before an agreed upon date. These fees will normally range from 0% to 8% depending on how long you have held the annuity at withdrawal. Surrender periods are usually between five and eight years. At this point the charges are usually eliminated."

"I like these strategies where we can get growth, but don't risk losing our money," Jason said.

"Exactly. You're seeing a pattern with these strategies we've discovered that allows you upside growth without the downside risk. That's what's so interesting about learning from the wealthy. They follow a set of rules for their investments, and one of those is to protect the principal.

"If that approach is good enough for millionaires and billionaires, why isn't it good enough for the average American trying to save for retirement?"

"It should be," Jason said, his wife nodding.

"Exactly. Success leaves clues, and if you follow those clues of the wealthy, you'll end up where they are—with financial independence."

"I really like that idea," Jason said. His mind kept going back to his grandma. He hated the idea of seniors being scammed and having nothing to live on. "401(k) plans don't have guaranteed income for life, do they?"

"No. 401(k)s don't offer lifetime income—they don't guarantee anything except for fees."

Private Real Estate Contracts

"Let's move to a really unique and exciting strategy. It may not be a good fit, but I'll share the basics with you just in case you want to learn more about it. It's something I personally have been using for years, and it's really been my family's hidden secret to creating exciting double-digit returns and financial independence. I learned this from my father, who's been doing it for about 30 years."

"Wow, so this is a secret family recipe, huh?" Jason asked.

"You could say that, although we're now teaching people about it because it's proven to be such a powerful wealth tool for us, and it works together with some of the other strategies we've already talked about. It's called 'private-lending contracts.'

"Private lending is actually a simple concept, but it's mysterious because it's not easy to do. Basically, it involves an individual who has money to lend and a borrower who needs cash. Some of the major benefits of private lending contracts are:

1. Good rates of return: You can achieve potential annual returns of 12-20% when done properly.

2. Managed risk and relative safety: While there is definitely risk involved, when you follow the process we share, you reduce your risk and have real property to back it up. What safety net do you have when paper stocks plummet?

3. Control of your money: You call the shots on where your money is invested—you don't depend on someone else to grow your money.

4. Low time commitment: Doing a deal can take as few as 6 hours, including paperwork and traveling to see the property. That's 6 hours to get 12%-20%. (There are circumstances when more time is required.)

5. Passive income: Your money is working for you whether you're in the Caribbean or taking a nap on Sunday afternoon! You don't trade hours for dollars anymore.

6. You can do it at any age: With qualified plans, there are all kinds of rules and red tape based on your age. Running a business can become more difficult the older you get. However, you can do private lending at any age because all you have to do is get in the car and go for a drive. My grandfather still does it, and he's in his 80s."

"Wow, that sounds pretty good," Jason said. "Yeah, I hear that a lot. Let me explain how it works so you can understand how you can get these benefits.

"A private-lending contract (PLC) is simply a private loan from one person to another. A traditional bank is not involved. This type of arrangement offers investors great returns and low risk when structured properly. The safety comes from securing the loan with collateral, typically a private residential home or commercial building.

Private-lending contracts have a higher interest rate than a bank because of supply and demand. Most people think higher interest rates equate to higher risk. That's typically true. However, the key to making this as secure as possible is to always lend on actual property and always be in first position on the loan."

"Why would anyone borrow money from a private money lender?" Susan asked.

"Good question. It's very simple. Banks have a certain appetite for risk. After 2008, they became even more conservative. Banks won't lend on properties like vacant land or short-term remodeling projects. When an investor sees a good deal, he needs to act fast. In many cases, the banks would never loan on these projects in the first place. Even if you *could* secure traditional financing, acquiring a loan from a bank usually takes a long time and a lot of red tape. In real estate, if you want to get a good deal, you need to act fast, and cash is king.

"This leaves a gaping hole for people who need money and can't acquire financing from a bank. This is where it becomes a win-win for private lenders and borrowers. Our clients don't lose out on a property that will be a good deal for them, and we earn a good interest rate.

"There's more risk to doing this than some of the other strategies, so you need to be very careful with the properties and the borrowers you work with.

"This is not 'no money down' real estate investing. Nor is it buying rental properties. Those may be good strategies, but that's not what we're talking about. This isn't a 'get rich quick' opportunity. However, you can grow your wealth much faster when your money is multiplying by up to 12% to 20% per year.

"Combining the strategies of private-lending Contracts with Financing Yourself To Wealth, which I'll show you in a minute, can amplify and multiply your wealth. Combining these strategies is what we call Double Arbitrage.

"Wow, look at the time. I've talked for too long and haven't even covered everything.

"We're always researching and bringing our Wealth Beyond Wall Street family new alternatives when we find them, so this list is by no means static. There are a couple more strategies we believe in that can give you good returns with more control of your money—I'll cover them quickly."

Entrepreneurship

"We've spoken about the 4th step in the Wealth Beyond Wall Street Framework being Multiply Your Wealth.

"This is not your 'typical' investing strategy, but I'm here because you want to learn how to create financial independence, right?"

"Right," Susan said.

"This last strategy is probably the single most proven and universally used method to create true wealth. In fact, there isn't a millionaire or billionaire I know of who hasn't used this to some degree.

"It's probably not what you're thinking because it's not your typical financial product or investing tool, but I don't want to hold anything back—this is something we're very serious about," Michael said.

"Of course, go ahead. I'd love to know," Jason said.

"Great. The 'strategy' millionaires and billionaires have used to create more wealth than any other single thing is ... business.

"At Wealth Beyond Wall Street, we believe that business is a great force for good in our world. It raises people out of poverty. It allows us to fulfill our potential, to create and innovate and improve the standard of living of ourselves and those around us. It creates jobs, and it supports and encourages people to achieve great things.

"Just look at how the standard of living in the entire world has skyrocketed in the past 200 years since America was created and free-market capitalism was allowed to work its magic in America and spread across the world. In fact, none of us would enjoy the many luxuries we have without entrepreneurs, innovators, and business owners willing to go out on a limb and risk their capital, their time, their careers, and their innovations to make the world a better place.

"So, something I would consider if you want to accelerate your wealth and have your net worth grow in multiples instead of just growing by percentage points each year is to have your own small (or large) business.

"At first, this sounds daunting to many people, but don't let your initial doubts kill this as an option before you get started. Because starting a business with low risk has never been easier! Approach it with an open mind, you can get started with a skill you already have, or you can sell a product you have access to that you can resell online. Amazon and eBay can do a large majority of the work for you. Increasing your income by $500 to $5000 per month can mean a world of difference for the average person, but when your business really gets going, the income can be truly life changing.

"It's impossible to build a home—or a mansion, for that matter—without raw materials. Your wealth is the same way. If you don't have enough extra money so you can put some into savings, your own business can be an answer.

On www.wealthbeyondwallstreet.com/amplifier you'll find a resource called the Income Amplifier that can help you if you want to pursue this on your own business after we're done here.

"The purpose of bringing this up today is not to derail our conversation about creating a better way to save money. Rather, it's to give you some food for thought on a time-tested method we have used, and many many others have used, to achieve financial independence.

"Now, one more important thing. Many of these strategies like annuities, precious metals, private-lending contracts, and even buying a franchise or starting a business can be done using money you have in qualified plans right now!

"If you have money tied up in a 401(k) or IRA and you don't want to lose a chunk of it in the next crash, there are options to access it in a self-directed IRA or other IRAs. That way, you can be in control of where that money is invested. Just make sure you check with your tax advisor before doing anything."

"Now let me share with you the most popular of the *Wealth Beyond Wall Street* strategies. It's the most popular because it really helps defeat all of the enemies of wealth we have discussed today. It provides 6 important benefits: First, you are guaranteed not to lose money in a market crash. Second, during good years you can grow your money potentially double digits to outpace inflation.

Third, experts call this the biggest benefit left in the tax code, because your money grows tax deferred, and you can access it tax free. Fourth, it can provide a supplemental retirement cash flow that could last until age 100. Fifth, you can use your money to become your own source of financing. Sixth, it is a self-completing policy, so if you pass away before you can save enough for your family to live on, the insurance benefit will provide the money needed."

"In very simple terms," Michael explains, "the IUL, short for Indexed Universal Life, is a customized cash value life insurance policy. In the next few minutes, I'm going to show you how it not only provides protection but can be a powerful wealth accumulation tool." We are spending time here because this is the foundation of the Wealth Beyond Wall Street strategy.

"Oh, no!" Susan cries. "Hold on! I've heard both Suze Orman and Dave Ramsey say that it's a bad idea to buy cash value life insurance!"

"Yeah," Jason chimes in. "My buddy who's a CPA says cash value life insurance is the wrong way to go. Lots of the financial pieces I've studied paint a poor picture of cash value life insurance, too. They say it's just too expensive."

"I'm going to debunk those myths for you in just a few minutes," Michael says, "and you're going to clearly see how cash value life insurance—*if* it's structured properly—can be a very solid solution for building wealth."

"Better than term insurance?" Jason asks.

"It's in a different league than term insurance," Michael says.

"Term insurance is important for one reason; to provide for

your family in the event of an untimely death. It's a bit like renting really. You rent the insurance for a set period of years, and after that term of 10 or 20 years is up, your insurance is gone. There's usually no equity in term policies. However, if you do happen to die during those years, your beneficiaries receive the death benefit from your policy."

Michael continues, "We, as Americans, spend more money insuring our cars than we do our lives. In fact, we actually do things in reverse: we focus on protecting the golden eggs—cars, homes, and other possessions—instead of protecting the goose that lays those golden eggs."

"I have to admit I'm guilty of that," Jason murmurs. "Pretty much all I've got is my little policy through work—a term policy—but, man, I sure shell it out on insurance for the cars and the house." Michael nods in understanding.

"Using cash value insurance like an IUL, can provide death benefit protection like term, along with a protected place for your money. It's sometimes referred to as *permanent* life insurance. And it's just what its name implies, too: it covers you until you die as long as you keep the policy in force. While we've all watched the stock market rise and fall, with banks and companies failing, the insurance industry has stayed solid. Did you know that during the Great Depression, while the banks and Wall Street crashed, the insurance industry not only maintained its strength, but kept its promises? During the Great Depression, clearly the greatest period of economic stress to date in the nation's history, policyholder cash values in life insurance companies were unaffected. Contrast that with the estimated 9,000-10,000 banks that failed during that time[26] and again in 2010, when over 143 banks failed[27]."

"Wow, I had no idea," Jason says.

"I like to look at history," Michael explains. "From the early 1930s until about 1980, life insurance companies—not Wall Street—were the dominant architects, builders, and custodians of the nation's savings and retirement systems.[28]

Jason splits the air with a low whistle. "I'm surprised—I really am. I didn't know any of that. But here's my question: my current policy, as I said, is term life. I've looked at prices, and, quite frankly, term is less money each month."

"Well, remember the reason we're here—it's not just to talk insurance. It's to show you how you could grow wealth without risking your money in stock market," Michael explains. "A term life policy usually doesn't provide any benefits to you while you're living. A permanent cash value life policy provides quite a few significant benefits to you while you're still alive. A term policy typically doesn't build cash value; whereas a permanent cash value life policy is designed to do exactly that."

"So why isn't everybody doing this?" Susan asks. "If cash value is so good, why haven't I heard more about it?"

"That's a very good question," Michael says. "As good as cash value insurance is, it's important to realize that all cash value policies don't work the same way. The criticisms targeted at permanent insurance often revolve around the fact that agents make large commissions on traditional policies. Also, too much of your money or yearly premiums go to buy insurance, instead of building cash value.

For the IUL, we've chosen companies that will allow you to max-fund the cash value side of the policy. Typically, this means that you can put as much money as possible toward your cash value and as little as possible toward the actual insurance costs.

The vast majority of financial professionals and insurance agents don't know how to do this properly to maximize the cash value growth. They've never been trained. You certainly don't get this advanced training when you study for your license! That's what makes working with me, a Wealth Beyond Wall Street professional, different; our specialty is to maximize your cash growth, not your insurance costs. Going this route typically cuts an agents commission in about half, but I gladly do it because it's better for my clients. Many agents don't see it this way, they'd rather double up the commission at the cost of the client…that is *not* how we do things.

The secret is not only working with an agent like me who understands how to build the policy correctly, but also in working with companies who support the concept," Michael explains.

Again, let's step back a moment from the story and review the key ingredients for building an IUL to accomplish what we have talked about. Here are a few of the most important pieces:

1. You want an insurance company with a long history of success and financial stability. One of the companies we work with has been in business for over 300 years and actually insured the home that Sir Isaac Newton lived in.

2. You need an agent who has been trained to create maximum cash value growth, without hurting your tax advantages.

3. You need a company who will allow you to maximize cash value growth, while minimizing your insurance costs. This is critical!

4. When you take a loan, your money can continue to grow as though you've never borrowed against your policy.

Let's say you buy the finest-quality chocolate bar available (representing term life insurance). You love chocolate and would like nothing more than to sink your teeth into that bar, but the people from whom you bought it say you can't do that. By law, you have to put it away. You can't touch it. It won't go to waste, though. As soon as you die, your heirs get to savor that chocolate bar on the way home from your funeral.

Who wants to buy a chocolate bar they can't even enjoy? You sure wouldn't want to pay much for it, would you? That's why term life is so popular: it costs less. In fact, it's the smallest amount of money you can invest and still provide *some* money for your heirs. But take a look at the reason it costs so much less—it's only in effect for a specified length of time, and it provides benefits only to your heirs. There's no benefit to you.

Okay, back to the chocolate bar metaphor. Now, say you buy the finest-quality chocolate bar available (representing cash value life insurance). This time, though, you're able to savor that chocolate bar while you're still alive. In fact, your chocolate bar keeps getting bigger and bigger—so not only do you get to *keep* enjoying it, but when you die, your heirs will have even more chocolate to enjoy together. And while they're enjoying the smooth sweetness, they'll do so with the satisfaction of knowing you enjoyed it, too.

"Basically, here's what happens," Michael explains. "You buy a properly structured cash value life policy that you agree to pay into each month. You are contractually promised a guaranteed amount of growth every year—even if you borrow from it and even when you take an income from it during retirement. You've got a predictable financial vehicle: it's guaranteed for life, and your principal is guaranteed, so you won't lose it during market swings. And you get what we call *living benefits* from an IUL."

There are actually several other wealth accumulation options you can use depending on your situation and your goals. There are also Income for Life options that can guarantee you never outlive your money. This can be a great peace of mind for folks going into retirement. There are also what we call "super charged" IULs that allow you to benefit f r o m the ups of market growth, without the risk. This is really exciting, and we'll cover it in a subsequent chapter.

From here on, when we—and Michael—talk about cash value insurance, we're talking about the kind of IUL that provides these powerful benefits to you—offered by the kind of companies we work with. Just about anyone can use it (you don't need to be educated or experienced), it can work on autopilot (you don't have to watch the market, reassess stocks based on performance or worry about tax consequences). And while it requires a bit of patience, it can work whether you have thousands or just a few hundred to set aside each month.

Now, let's get back to the story.

Chapter 9:

FINANCE YOURSELF TO WEALTH

"Those who understand interest earn it, those who don't, pay it."

—Albert Einstein

"So far it's sounding pretty good," says Susan, "but what do you mean by *living benefits?*"

"I've already mentioned a few," Michael responds. "The IUL gives you protection that is guaranteed by the insurance company that your principal is immune from whatever the stock market is doing. Another benefit is taxes. The IRA expert Ed Slott says, "Life insurance is the single biggest benefit to the IRS tax code."[29] You save taxes on the growth of your principal, you can access the cash value without paying taxes and when the death benefit is paid out to your heirs it comes to them income tax free in most cases because you paid taxes on the money before you put it into your policy.

And remember that one of the risks of 401(k) plans and mutual funds is the risk that the government could change the rules midstream due to the latest political agenda or bureaucratic whim," Michael says. "With an IUL, your policy is a private contract between you and the insurance company. "

"Of course one of the greatest living benefits is your ability to reduce or totally stop paying interest to banks and Finance Yourself to Wealth™," Michael explains.

"How does that work?" Jason asks.

"We'll use a car for example. Let's say you want to buy a $20,000 car. You can get a loan from a bank or car financing company, or in your case, use your IUL to finance the car.

.With traditional car financing you might finance the car for five years or so. In the end you have a car paid off and you've lost all the interest and principal to the finance company.

When you Finance Yourself to Wealth™, you borrow against the cash value in your IUL and pay for the car in cash. (Often paying cash can save you money on the purchase price by itself.) Then you make payments back to your policy. This is where it gets exciting—after the five years, you've got your car paid off, but you also have the $20,000 back into your IUL!

Plus, you can pay additional interest with your payments and the extra money will go to increase your cash value. This is why we call it Financing Yourself to Wealth™. Because each time you take out a loan and pay it back with extra interest, it actually increases your cash value."

"That sounds interesting!" Susan says.

"With a cash value insurance policy," Michael continues, "you have access to the cash value in your policy, and you can't be turned down for a loan. If you need to borrow the cash value from your policy, just say the word. No credit check, no tax returns, no qualifying hassle. And no one's going to raise your interest rate if you're late on a payment. In fact, *you* determine the repayment timetable, and *you* decide how often and for how long you want to make payments."

"This almost sounds too good to be true," Jason says.

"It gets even better," Michael responds. "Remember when we talked about how one of the enemies of wealth is interest? When you use your IUL to finance your purchases, your money continues to grow at the same rate, as though you never touched a dime. When you pay the loan back you recoup the cost of that purchase back into your policy, rather than making payments to someone else. You can enjoy some of the things you'd like without destroying your nest egg."

By this time, Jason and Susan are both wide-eyed. "There's got to be a hitch," Susan says, "and I can think of a big one. I'm not sure we'd even qualify for insurance right now. I just had some really serious health problems."

"If you're too old or have health issues that might make you uninsurable, you're not out of luck," Michael explains. "You can buy a policy on a child, spouse or grandchild who does qualify to be insured. You own the policy, and you still control it so you decide what happens to the money. So let's assume you can qualify. If your policy is structured properly, your policy is permanent. That means as long as you keep it in force, it will be with you forever. This is extremely important when it comes to taxes. Life insurance is one of the best estate tax planning vehicles there is because it gets paid to your estate income tax free.

Michael adds, "That's another one of the great benefits: your life is insured. The average man in this country has an economic value of more than $1 million dollars. If you die, especially if you die early, your family could suffer a significant economic loss on top of the emotional sorrow of losing you. Insurance provides financially for those you leave behind. In fact, as long as it's in force, your policy will generally pay out a lump-sum income tax-free death benefit that's far larger than the total premiums."

"Now keep in mind, as we're referencing Financing Yourself to Wealth™ we're talking about policy loans, not withdrawals. Withdrawals are when you permanently take the money out of the policy. The reason why we use loans is because your money continues to grow, even while you are using it. Then, as you pay it back, it is there for you to use again and again."

"So what happens if we can't pay the loans back?" asks Susan.

"The idea is to be able to structure the loans so they can be paid back, similar to a regular car loan. If, for some reason, you can't make payments for a while, it's not a huge deal. No one will be knocking on your door to collect. You simply resume paying when you can. However, you definitely want to pay the loans back if you are using them for Financing Yourself to Wealth™."

"But what happens if we can't for some reason?" Susan asks.

"You will continue to pay interest on the loan, and ultimately the policy could cancel.[30] Just like gardening—if you stop watering a plant, it stops growing. We want to keep nurturing the IUL so it continues to grow. Then once you hit your retirement years, we can structure your policy so it is paid up and you never have to pay more into it. It can then be there to provide retirement income."

"But," Michael says. "Here's the real beauty of a loan from your policy: *you* structure the repayment schedule. *You* determine how much you can pay and how often you want to pay.

"Makes sense, but is there a limit to how much we can put in?" Jason asks.

"Yes," Michael says. "We want to make sure that your policy doesn't become a Modified Endowment Contract (MEC). In order to enjoy the maximum tax benefits of your IUL, you want to keep the policy within the MEC limit.

The IRS has set up guidelines that dictate how much cash value you can put into a policy compared to the insurance amount. If you exceed their limits, meaning you put in too much cash, it could have negative tax implications—essentially ruining one of the major benefits for getting an IUL. As Wealth Beyond Wall Street agents, we are trained on how to structure the policy so you stay under the MEC limit to enjoy maximum tax advantages.

"Yeah," Jason replies, "I can see why we want to work with someone who's been trained to do this properly. I'd hate to lose out on tax savings just because of an untrained agent."

"If this is so great," Susan chimes in, "why haven't I heard anything about it? Is it because it's new?"

"Absolutely not," Michael answers. "In fact, Americans have been using permanent life insurance policies for over 100 years. Large companies, business people and average citizens protect their capital by buying cash value life insurance policies on their employees and then using these cash value life insurance policies as strong foundations. One reason why you might not have heard about it is that gurus, bankers and Wall Street have no interest in promoting these policies because they often want you to invest in the market."

"Okay," Jason nods. "So how do we get started?"

"The bottom line is this," Michael explains. "You can start by funding an IUL, a special type of cash value insurance life policy. Then, instead of borrowing from a bank, you borrow from your policy. You simply use a different way to pay for things—a method that lets you recoup the cost of large purchases, instead of letting that money goes into a lenders pocket. And all the while you're growing a tidy nest egg, one you can predict and, even better, one you can count on. In fact, that's why we created the quiz on www.wealthbeyondwallstreet.com/quiz to give you your Never Work Again Number."

"That *sounds* good," Susan agrees, "but I'm not sure I understand. Why not just put my money in an interest-bearing savings account and then use that money to buy the things I want? Wouldn't I actually come out ahead in the long run?"

"First," Michael replies, "how much does your money grow in a bank account while you aren't using it for something else? 1.5 - 2%, if you are lucky? If you invest in a bond or CD, the percentage of growth will be a little higher. Now consider this: with an IUL, not only can your money grow at a guaranteed rate, but if you structure it right—and as a Wealth Beyond Wall Street professional, I know how to do it right—you could also receive growth when the market goes up, without risking your money in the market."

"But here's the part of the answer that's really convincing," Michael continues. "Let's say you deposit your money in a bank account, and then withdraw the $20,000 we talked about to pay cash for a car. Does the bank continue to pay you interest on the money you withdrew? Of course not. But guess what? Your IUL policy *does.* That's the amazing thing about an IUL. People really think it is too good to be true, yet it is true, and it can be a great financial tool for those who take advantage of it."

"I've got to admit I'm pretty stunned by all this."

Jason says, "I just went through a pretty big hassle with the 401 (k) deal—are there rules here? I mean, what kinds of things can I borrow money for?"

"You can borrow from your account for anything you want," Michael answers. "You can run many of your large purchases through it—cars, vacations, business expenses, home improvement and even real estate purchases. It's your money, and no one's going to tell you what you can do with it."

"So, it's like our own source of financing," Susan says. "But we set the terms and have more control over it."

"Exactly," says Michael. "In the end, what your IUL policy really can give you is a solid foundation. A foundation for your overall financial plan that you can count on without risking your principal or worrying about what the market is doing or getting access to your money if something comes up. It's a predictable and protected way to put away your money. Following this approach could ultimately create millions of dollars in wealth for you and your family, while at the same time allowing you to reduce the amount of interest you are paying to banks."

The relief on Jason's face is obvious. "After what we've been through, this would really allow me to sleep well at night," he says.

"Absolutely." Michael responds. "You don't even have to wait until you retire. You get to enjoy the benefits now. For example, if you want to take a family vacation next year, just get started now. When the time comes, you pull out a couple thousand dollars and go. Then pay the loan back and you recoup the cost of that vacation and it's there for you when you need it next time."

"So we can use it for the kitchen remodel we're thinking of doing too, huh?" says Susan.

"Absolutely," Michael replies. "Home improvement, college, cars, even investing in a business or real estate—whatever you want. Then when you're ready to retire, you can take withdrawals and loans without having to pay taxes on that money as long as it is structured properly."

"I'm pretty much sold," Jason says, and Susan nods. "But as you can imagine, we don't have a lot of cash on hand right now. How much do we have to invest to get started?"

"The cost to you is only the amount you want to pay in premiums," Michael says. "There are several different ways to get started. Some folks redirect savings from current income, some move part of their savings sitting in the bank over, in fact there are many different ways to find money to fund an IUL. There's no determined amount you have to start with."

"But we have to make monthly premium payments, right?" asks Susan.

"Not necessarily," says Michael. "It's very flexible. You could pay all up front, pay yearly, or even set up what I call an "automatic wealth building machine". This would automatically transfer money from your bank account and pay your premiums each month without you worrying about it. But I imagine the real question you were trying to ask is how you're going to come up with the extra money. That's something specific I want to talk over with you. There are quite a few places I can help you find money to fund your policy. I'm confident that you can easily—and probably painlessly—divert money from other sources to build your cash value without changing your lifestyle. Let's start with the most obvious: how much money do you get back on tax returns each year?"

Jason says, "About $4,000 - $5,000."

"Okay, so that's about $400 extra dollars every month you are sending to the IRS for no reason. Is there a reason you like to let Uncle Sam use your money for 12 months without paying you a dime of interest on it?"

"Well, when you put it like that, no I guess it's not a good idea is it? I just don't want to have to pay extra when the tax time comes around," Jason finishes.

"I understand. It's easy to set your deductions so that you still get a small refund, while allowing most of your money to stay with you to use throughout the year. If you add up the $4,000 - $5,000 for the next 15-20 years of your working life that could be an extra $100,000 you could add to your cash value."

"Well sheesh," Susan breaks in, "We should do that immediately!"

"We can build a policy that works for you. One client bought cash value policies on each of his boys when they were very young. At the time, his intention was to accumulate some cash, but to also provide them with death benefit coverage when they became adults and responsible for their individual families. As it turns out, one is now married with one daughter. He has cash value that can be used for his daughter's college expenses, braces, family vacations or new cars. The young son, who is still single, has cash value to continue his college degree, replace his vehicle when the time comes or make a down payment on a home."

"So we could set these up for our kids as well?" Susan asks.

"Yes. In fact, once you get your own IUL in place, many people end up with multiple policies in the family. Kids can use them for a college funding options, or to pay for their first car or house." Michael replies.

"So, once we get started, can we start using the money right away, or do we have to wait?" Jason asks.

"Usually you can access your cash value within a couple of weeks. You could use it right away to fund that remodeling project you've been talking about."

"It's important to realize that an IUL is not a get-rich-quick scheme," emphasizes Michael. "It's a long term approach to put you on the path to becoming wealthy outside Wall Street. It requires diligence and patience."

"You keep talking about becoming a millionaire. If using your approach we were able to cut back on some of the areas we're currently wasting, change my withholdings so I keep more of my tax money throughout the year, and redirect my $550 per month 401(k) contributions over…that's… about $400 per month on taxes, $550 on our 401(k) and we're wasting another $50 per month right now on extra landline phone we don't use…

So how much could we have if we put about $1000 per month into a policy?" Jason asks.

"Good question, this is the beauty of the IUL—it allows us to put money away and know, with relative certainty, how much is going to be there for you when you need it."

Susan chimes in. "Yeah, I'm really tired of opening our 401(k) statement and seeing it go down, down, down!"

"Usually an IUL performs best the longer you let it grow and compound. When do you think you will want to start taking money out?" Michael asks.

"Well, let's say age 65," Jason replies.

After crunching a few numbers Michael says, "Assuming that you get average growth of 7-8% using the indexing strategy (we'll cover this in a second) at the age of 65 you could have right around $643,000 with a death benefit of approximately $929,000 that could go to your spouse or children. But here's the real exciting part…are you ready?[31]"

"Yeah what have you got?"

"Using these projections, at age 65, you could have an annual cash flow that you access without a taxable event, of $86,000 until age 100."

"$86,000 per year…that I get without a taxable event? Wow, that's amazing…especially considering it's not going to get wiped out in a market downturn, and we know we can count on it being protected," Susan says.

"$86,000 per year for 35 years is like 3 million dollars! How is that possible?" Jason says.

"Remember that when you borrow against your policy, the cash value continues to grow as if it's never been touched. It's also important to remember these projections are done using the insurance company's actuarial projections. They use data from the past 25 years …but they aren't guaranteed. There's a chance it could be less than that."

Susan jumps in "I appreciate you saying that, I hate to be sold a bill of goods only to be disappointed. Even if it's half that amount, having about $43,000 per year to live on until age 100 is pretty fantastic. Plus, that money isn't at risk in the market."

"$1000 might be pushing it for us right now, what would happen if we only did say $500 per month?" Susan asks.

"No problem," Michael says "With $500 per month, you're still potentially looking at $43,000 every year until age 100. The reason you don't pay tax on this money is because you are borrowing against the policy, not withdrawing the money out of the policy.

Of course this is the way it works under current IRS tax laws."

"Keep in mind," continues Michael, "these policies work with compound interest. Meaning the more money you put into your policy, the faster your policy grows. Why wouldn't you want to put as much money as possible into a policy that only gets better the more you put in? With traditional financial tools like 401(k)'s or mutual funds, there is no direct correlation between the amount you contribute and improving results. An IUL gets better as you add more. In fact the growth maximizes when you need it most during your later years."

"Interesting. So we should consider finding ways to increase the amount we pay in because we'll get better results that way?" Susan asks.

"Exactly," Michael adds. "Plus, don't forget that you can access that money without having to pay taxes on it under the current IRS tax codes—and as long as you structure the policy correctly. That's why working with a trained Wealth Beyond Wall Street professional is so important. If you don't do it right, you could lose major tax benefits or miss out on maximizing your cash value growth. This is too important to trust to someone who hasn't had the proper training."

As we step away from the table, it is clear that Jason and Susan are off to a good start on their journey to becoming wealthy outside the Wall Street casino. But, as we leave them to the beginning of their new financial life, we have some shocking revelations to show you.

In the next chapter, we'll show you what might just be the most exciting part of this whole process.

Part of the reason why Jason and Susan can potentially have such a great cash flow in retirement, is because they are using the Indexing strategy with an IUL. This allows them to benefit when the market goes up... but never risk their money to loss when it comes down! That's exactly what you'll see in the next chapter.

How to Find Money to Fund an IUL

1. **I'll have that back, thank you.**
   How much is your tax refund each year? Think about changing your deductions to keep more of your income instead of letting the IRS use it for a full year before giving it back to you.

2. **Redirect your cash flow.**
   Often you can redirect money currently going into poorly performing or risky market investments into an IUL.

3. **Make your money go to work for you.**
   Often funding a policy with extra money you've got in the bank makes sense because you are getting guaranteed growth and still have access to it.

4. **Get off the roller coaster.**

   This may be a no-brainer if you have money in stocks or mutual funds. Consider moving some money out of the market if you are tired of the roller coaster.

5. **Stop the expenses.**
   When they add it all up, people are often shocked at how much extra they are paying in insurance, utilities and other every day expenses. Making some minor lifestyle changes, or just doing a little research on reducing current expenses can help you build up your cash value and get on the path of the wealthy.

continued on next page...

continued from previous page

6. **In force insurance policies.**

   Many people have existing life insurance policies that are not structured as effectively as possible. You may be able to do a 1035 exchange that keeps the cash value and the tax benefits you currently have, while improving your results.

7. **Chopping away at debt.**

   Instead of slowly chopping away at debt, consider funding an IUL and then taking a chunk of money and paying off the balance of a credit card. This could save you a substantial amount on interest costs.

8. **Splurge on your future.**

   Instead of taking the money from your tax return and buying that big screen TV or trip, consider funding an IUL and building on your financial future.

9. **Extra mortgage payments.**

   If you are currently making extra payments to your mortgage principal, consider putting that into an IUL where growth is guaranteed while also giving you access to that cash without having to qualify for a loan in order to use it.

   To download a free copy of the Found Money Checklist, go to **www.wealthbeyondwallstreet.com.**

Chapter 10

SUPER CHARGING
THE IUL

"The first rule of investing is NEVER LOSE MONEY.
The second rule is NEVER forget rule #1."

—Warren Buffett

I've always wanted to fly. Not in a plane, hot air balloon or with the help of something man made. I simply want to look up and take off flying through the air. Unfortunately, I haven't figured out how to make that happen—like the old saying goes: "What goes up must come down."

I learned that the hard way jumping off the bunk bed as a kid.

As we've discussed, this up and down phenomenon is not limited to physics—it happens quite frequently in the stock market as well. We can have some exhilarating rides up only to suffer financial broken bones when the market comes crashing back down. But it doesn't have to be that way. In this chapter I'm going to show you how you may just be able to defy market gravity.

One of the most exciting things about an IUL is that you can supercharge the cash value portion of your insurance policy by using a special indexing strategy. The indexing strategy can allow you to enjoy the upside growth of the market without ever risking your money to market losses! (You can go up without coming down!)

In other words, the indexing strategy could give you double-digit returns on up years when the market gains without the downside risk!

This means when the market goes up, your money can grow (I'll explain more in just a second) *but when the market goes down, you are protected and your money cannot be lost.* This can be extremely beneficial during times of market turbulence. In years when the market goes up, so do your cash values, and when the market falls, you are protected against that loss. Your money is locked in so you don't lose!

Now, why is this so important?

Because inflation is one of the biggest threats to growing your money and wealth. If inflation is running at 3-5% (or even higher depending on the government's monetary policy) it's important to have your money outpace inflation.

If your money is growing slower than the rate of inflation, you aren't growing your money—you are actually decreasing the value of it over time! The indexing strategy can allow you to outpace inflation by capitalizing on potential double-digit growth in the years when the market goes up.

Wait a minute. Didn't I just spend several of the first chapters in this book explaining why the stock market may not be the greatest place to invest your money? Am I changing my tune?

Not at all.

The cash value growth in your indexed universal life policy is *linked to the S&P 500* but your cash is *not* actually invested *in* the market. That way, your money is always guaranteed by the insurance company.

Remember in Chapter 2 when we showed you the different plunges the market had taken over the years and how long it took to recover and return to even? Now you don't have to deal with that at all!

Your money is protected from any market loss, because it is not directly in the market, but at the same time, you benefit from the growth of the S&P 500 up to a limit or cap. Let's say the upside cap is 12% (This can vary from policy to policy). This means even if the market goes up 14% or more, your cash value growth would be limited to just 12%.

Having a cap is actually a good thing because this is what allows the insurance company to protect you against losses in those years when the market goes down.

Let's look at a picture that will illustrate this point. This is a hypothetical example of a typical stock market strategy vs. an index strategy.

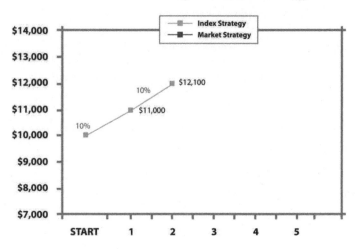

So, let's say you start out with $10,000. And in the first year the S&P 500 grows by 10%. The first year, there is no difference, and you have $11,000 in either account. In year two your money grows another 10%. Now you have $12,100 in either account.

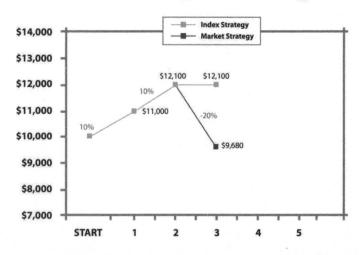

But let's say that in year three the S&P 500 drops 20%. Can that happen? Sure it can. The last few years of the 2000s were worse times than that! Now you would have about $9,600 if had you invested directly in the S&P 500. However, in the indexed strategy, your principal and interest are protected against market loss. So, now instead of $9,600, you hold at $12,100.

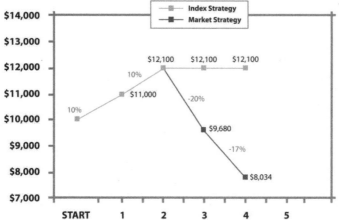

In year four the market drops another 17%. Now, instead of having $9,600, you have around $8,034. In the indexed strategy, you're still on hold at $12,100.

Now here's the million-dollar question: Do you want $8,034 or $12,100?

That's quite a difference, and it's clear from this example that losing principal can be financially devastating. That's why Warren Buffet said "it's not so much about the return *on* your money as the return *of* your money." When you lose principal, you've got to get big time results to bring it back to even.

Now let's look at what happens when the market rebounds. Let's say in year five the market grows by 15%. In the stock market strategy, the $8,034 would get the full 15% growth, which is about $1,205, so your cash value would climb back up to a little over $9,239. In the indexed strategy, your money would only grow by 12% (remember we have a cap) to $13,552. But even with the capped growth, you have $13,552 versus $9,239! Again, quite a difference.

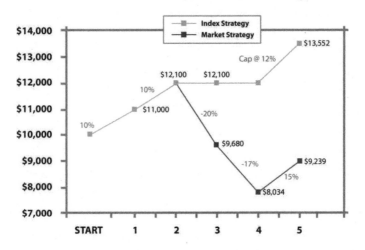

Index Strategy vs. Market Strategy

In this example, the downsides of the stock market strategy were:

✓ After five years, you end up with less money than you started with.

✓ It will take a 25% return to get you back to your original $10,000 (and how likely is that to happen in *one* year?)

✓ Even if you did get the 25% you needed, it will only bring you back to $10,000. You just lost *five* years and you are just barely back to even.

Can you see why the indexing strategy is so exciting? Now you can have your money growing when the market goes up, you could outpace inflation with potential double-digit gains, and you never have to worry about losing money when the market goes down.

What kind of peace of mind would that give you—knowing that your money is protected from market crashes?

Now what would happen if the market goes down for 10 years in a row?

Many of the IUL policies can be set up so that there is a guaranteed amount of growth credited to your policy cash values, which guarantees that even if you don't achieve growth in the index, your cash value can continue to grow. (Every policy is a little bit different. That's why it's so important to work with a trained Wealth Beyond Wall Street professional who can show you your options.)

The rest of the IUL benefits still work the same. Meaning, you can Finance Yourself to Wealth™ by accessing your cash value for cars, college or other major purchases. *Some financial products can even guarantee an income you will never outlive.* Be sure to ask your Wealth Beyond Wall Street professional about this!

Now with all this being said, indexed life insurance doesn't have to be where you put all your money, but for many people, it is an excellent way to position a portion of your portfolio to enjoy the ups of the market without the downside risk.

This is obviously a brief introduction to the indexing strategy to learn more about how this works, just request a Blueprint at the end of this book and a Wealth Beyond Wall Street professional can help you see it in action and answer your questions.

The Wrap

The indexed strategy makes sense for people who want to avoid market risk, but still want the possibility of double-digit gains and all the other benefits that an IUL can give them.

Using this strategy you could save more money even without changing your current lifestyle by repositioning some of your assets from being deposited into accounts that are taxed during retirement to an indexed life insurance policy.

The supercharged indexing strategy could allow you to:

✓ Benefit from double-digit gains in up years

✓ Help outpace inflation

✓ Grow your money tax deferred

✓ Access cash values without incurring tax

✓ Provide cash flow for life

In the next chapter, we'll show you exactly how cash value life insurance impacted the lives of men and women just like yourself. And you'll also recognize some of the biggest names in business that used their cash value life insurance to build their wealth.

Turn the page to see if you recognize a few of these people who, like many of our own policy holders, used the living benefits of life insurance to growth their wealth.

To maximize your growth and give you all the advantages described here, an IUL should be from a life insurance company that meets these requirements:

1. Cash max structure; to maximize cash value and minimize insurance costs

2. 2% guaranteed growth on cash values

3. Flexible loans; so you can switch from variable to fixed loan and back

4. Participating Loans; so your money participates in the growth of the index even when you have a loan on the policy.

5. Loyalty bonus on cash values at year 10

6. Decreasing or disappearing charges

7. Very Strong Financially; confirmed by independent rating services

8. Cap that allows *double digit* growth in good years

9. 100% Participation Rate; so your cash value grows dollar for dollar when the index grows; (up to the cap).

Section 4

EXAMPLES IN ACTION

*People seldom improve when they have
no other model but themselves to copy after.*

—Oliver Goldsmith

Chapter 11

DISNEY, J.C. PENNEY, MCDONALD'S AND YOU; MAKING IT WORK

*"Though no one can go back and make a brand new start,
anyone can start from now and make a brand new ending."*

—Carl Bard

Holly is a 42-year-old New Yorker and a single mother of two.

She has a steady job working in an HR department, making about $33,000 per year and is having a hard time making ends meet.

Her two kids are in the "expensive" stage of life—middle school and high school—where it seems like every time you turn around there's another expense to pay for.

She's running ragged taking care of two kids, working full-time, paying the bills and keeping the house in order.

It's almost too much for any one person to handle.

Add to it the fact that she's in a seemingly insurmountable amount of debt, and Holly doesn't feel like she's ever going to get out of the hole she's in.

She sees no light at the end of the tunnel—no way out!

But it gets worse.

She was actually in more debt than even she realized. After totaling up all the credit cards, lines of credit with stores and the student loans, her debt total, not including her car or home, was over $59,000.

She knew it was bad, but this was a real eye opener. That was two years' worth of her salary, and $59,000 did not even count her car or home debt.

She was contributing $100 per month to a company retirement plan, but she knew that was not going to give her the financial independence she wanted.

The rest of her paycheck each month was going to pay bills or pay down credit card and student loan debt.

Not surprisingly, when we asked her what three financial goals she had, her reply was a lot like you might guess.

First, she'd like to have a little money set aside to take a break and breathe for a weekend or so.

Next, she wants to get out of debt and have some emergency savings put away just in case something comes up with her or her children.

And lastly, she wants to be able to save money for her kid's college funds and her own retirement.

With only $33,000 of income, $59,000 in consumer debt and college loans, two kids and a mortgage—doesn't this seem like a hopeless case?

Left to her own devices, she really was. She didn't know what to do, and she didn't feel there was any way out of her current situation.

That's where we came in. After reviewing her debts, expenses and current retirement contributions, we helped Holly put together an I U L, which included a spending and a debt analysis. Through that process, we helped Holly find and put away over $500 per month that she was currently wasting!

Over $500 per month on just a $33,000 per year salary!

With our specialized help, she discovered money in multiple areas that she was currently wasting.

Plus, she was able to redirect her current retirement contributions that were currently at risk in the market into an indexed universal life insurance policy to create a nest egg she can count on. She is literally started down the path to becoming wealthy without risking her money!

This might seem hard to believe, but the exciting part is that based on the insurance company projections, by the time she turns 65, she could potentially take out $68,000 per year, every year until age 100! Plus, as long as she does it properly, that money can be accessed without incurring tax!

Imagine her relief when we gave her the IUL Blueprint that showed her how, using just her current income, she could create a simple strategy to follow.

This process helped her get out of debt, get her spending under control and ultimately, gave her hope because she now has a blueprint for financial independence.

By steadily putting away money each month, she could have the security of knowing that after age 65, she could have as much as $68,000 per year on just a $33,000 income! Plus, when she does pass on, she'll have a death benefit payable to her two children because of her life insurance policy!

JC Penney

In 1898, James Cash Penney was working in a Golden Rule Store, which was one shop in a small chain of dry goods stores. He turned out to be such an enterprising worker that the pair of owners took him under their wing, offering him a one-third partnership in a new store they were opening. James managed to scrape together $2,000—a pretty significant sum in those days—and opened the new store in Kemmerer, Wyoming.

During the next five years, James helped open two more stores and was doing very well. James focused his efforts on the stores, even investing the extra money that he made by working as a lumberjack into them. By 1912 he was running 34 stores throughout the Rocky Mountain region.

The next year, James moved his company headquarters to Salt Lake City, Utah and incorporated under a name you'll easily recognize: The J.C. Penney Company. The J.C. Penney chain exploded and by 1929 there were 1,400 stores throughout the nation.

Then things got interesting. The stock market crashed, and the nation was plunged into the depths of the Great Depression.

The depression devastated his stores and his wealth. He was in financial ruin.

Luckily James had not risked all of his money in the market. He had built a cash value insurance foundation. To rebound from the difficult times, he took out a loan from his cash value life insurance policies. He used the cash to meet day-to-day and payroll expenses for his chain of stores. Not only did he keep his head above water, but he also rebounded. Today, the stores take in revenues nationwide of $18.5 billion a year.

As it turns out, that simple cash loan had a greater impact than even James could have realized. Ever heard of Wal-Mart? On a 1940 visit to a J.C. Penney store in Des Moines, Iowa, James patiently trained a young employee, Sam Walton, showing him how to gift-wrap packages using the least amount of ribbon needed to do the job—and later another retail giant was born.

Doctor Jeff

Jeff thought he was doing pretty well.

He was in his late forties, making a great income as a doctor, and putting $1,000 into his 401(k) every month.

On top of that, Jeff had over $110,000 already socked away. Of course, he wasn't really thrilled that he'd recently lost a big chunk of it in the market crash of 2008, yet despite this setback, *he thought he was still on track for a great lifestyle.*

He wanted financial independence at age 60, and he figured if he could have $70,000-$80,000 per year to live for the rest of his life, he could hang it up whenever he wanted to after 60. He was also afraid inflation was going to continue to eat away at his savings.

Jeff wanted to make sure that he could provide his own retirement cash flow. He didn't want to count on social security because, according to the Congressional Budget Office, in 2011 the Social Security Administration was already running a 45 Billion dollar deficit. And at the end of the day, he wanted to be in control of his finances and retirement, not risk it to someone else.

You could say Jeff thought he had it all under control. In his mind, he was doing everything right; until he saw the truth.

You see, most people have no idea how long their money will actually last after they stop working.

Jeff crunched some quick numbers. He already had $110,000 saved, plus he was adding $1,000 per month to his 401(k). The result was shocking. He discovered that if he continued on his current path, he would only have about $30,000 per year during retirement. And this was BEFORE taxes! Assuming he's in a 20% tax bracket, that's more like $23,400 per year or $2,000 per month!

Right now Jeff is living off $10,000 per month, so living off just $2,000 per month was like a cold bucket of water right in the face.

But that's not all.

There are other problems with Jeff's current plan.

The money in his current retirement plan is fully taxable, like we already showed above; the $30,000 gets taxed when he pulls it out to use it. Plus, if he dies before he retires, his income stops and he won't have the money built up to provide his wife or family—there are no guarantees or death benefit. The money is at risk in the market, and the money is tied up in a qualified government plan.

But it gets worse.

This is what really shocked him: For his 80th birthday present, he would be looking at an empty retirement account! That's right, his $2,000 per month would be gone by the time he's 80.

Remember, Jeff wants to retire at age 60. Using the Lifestyle Income Estimator on our website, we showed him that his $2,000 per month could actually run out in less than 20 years!

According to US News and World Report, once a man reaches 65-years-old, life expectancy is 83-years-old and one in every four will live past age 90.[32]

He wondered what type of lifestyle he was going to have with just $2,000 per month, living with the fear that the money would run out all too soon.

So, we looked at some other options for him.

By using an IUL and working with a Wealth Beyond Wall Street professional—one that specializes in helping people build cash flow that they won't outlive—we came up with a solution that excited and delighted him.

Jeff wanted to see what his retirement would look like if he redirected the $1,000 a month into an indexed cash value insurance policy.

He was comfortable using one of our IUL Insurance Companies because this particular one has been around for over 100 years and has hundreds of billions of dollars in assets around the globe.

After implementing the indexing strategies, Jeff was amazed and excited at his new financial independence blueprint.

Remember, in his current situation he was looking at running out of money after 15 to 20 years. Plus, this income was fully taxable, didn't have any guarantees and it was at risk in the market.

With the Indexed policy, his new strategy could give him approximately $69,000 per year—for the rest of his life! And as long as he follows the IRS code properly, he could access that cash flow without a taxable event (according to current IRS tax code).

But that's not all.

In his new IUL, he has no market risk, and if he dies too soon his family will be protected with the life insurance death benefit. Plus, he has access to the cash value in his insurance policy to Finance Himself to Wealth™ throughout his life!

Like we mentioned before, Jeff was excited about $70,000 per year compared to $24,000…and delighted when he saw this new prospect. Wouldn't you be?

What if you are already in your late fifties or even sixties and don't have a situation like Jeff has. Is it too late?

Thankfully it's not. There are still many options for people of any age, but it's important to start now, and not let another day go by without implementing the strategies that you have learned here. Get started at www.wealthbeyondwallstreet.com today.

Walt Disney

The second household name you'll no doubt recognize, involves a man who fought all odds to follow his dream: Walt Disney.[33] Walt and his brother, Roy, were in the animation business. Their story is almost too hard to believe. One of their most popular characters was stolen by another studio. Their best animator jumped ship. Their studio was chronically understaffed and almost always in debt. In fact, Walt Disney struggled financially for years on the brink of bankruptcy—actually going bankrupt at the age of 21.

Fast-forward to the early 1950s. The only amusement parks in the entire country were horrifically dilapidated places peppered with rusting, creaky rides and known only for their filthy restrooms and the drunks that always hung around. Walt dreamed instead of an immaculately clean amusement park filled with imaginative rides—a place where families weren't afraid to eat the food. World War II had just ended, and the nation was licking its wounds. Walt dreamed of creating an amusement park with an idealistic Main Street, U.S.A., where families could identify with something wholesome and good. But that's not all: he dreamed of charging admission to his park and actually making a profit.

Everyone to whom he presented his idea thought he was crazy—and told him so. After all, *no one* charged admission to an amusement park. That just wasn't done. And amusement parks simply couldn't be family-friendly; everyone knew you'd have to sell alcohol if you had a prayer of staying afloat. Even his brother Roy—also his business partner and financial manager—told him it couldn't be done. He urged Walt to forget it. After all, they were in the animation business, not the amusement park business.

Determined to achieve his dream, Walt had no choice but to move ahead on his own. Turned down by traditional financing, he emptied his savings account, sold his vacation home in Palm Springs and recruited the help of a few employees who shared his vision. Then, he used a loan from his cash value insurance policies to help finance the park. (Roy later admitted he had no idea where Walt's money was coming from but decided not to ask.)

What happened to Walt's dream? Disneyland opened on September 8, 1955, with 18 attractions. It welcomed half a million visitors in the first month it was open. By the end of its first year, it had hosted more than 3.5 million guests. Less than three years later, it welcomed its ten millionth visitor—a number that exceeded well-known national landmarks like Yellowstone and the Grand Canyon. Today, its California Park alone— with more than 60 attractions—has been visited by more than 600 million guests from throughout the world. A dozen of the original attractions from 1955 are still operating in the park today, as a testament to Walt Disney's dream of a high-quality, enduring adventure for families.

Stephen G.

Stephen distinctly remembers the day he first knew that nothing could stop him. He had landed a great paying sales job, and he was also less than a year away from graduating with a degree in business. He was finally on his way up.

It had been a busy year for Stephen. In fewer than 12 months, he had sold his old home—for a tidy profit—and finished building his family's new home. Just as they were unpacking the boxes, his wife announced that they were expecting a baby. They were delighted! Stephen knew life would change, and that his cost of living would go up with another mouth to feed, but the idea of his growing family only motivated him to work all the harder.

Life seemed to be moving in the right direction for Stephen.

He'd been with the company for almost a year when the recession of 2008 caused the economy to plummet. The medical specialty that Stephen served was hit particularly hard. Things started to get tough. His income was going down but his costs weren't.

With his wife at home, caring for their new baby, and with only one income to support the family, money became tight for the first time in their marriage.

Stephen went from comfort and a sense of security to just the opposite. In just 12 months he went from having $15,000 in the bank to having $15,000 in credit card debt. He went from the joy of building a new home to the fear of losing that home. He went from a feeling of being unstoppable to a gripping sensation of worry. He despaired of ever being able to climb out of debt and replace his savings.

Stephen now had an empty bank account, a whopping credit card debt, two ailing cars, and a home on the verge of being foreclosed. He faced the embarrassment of losing his house, disappointing his family and starting over. The last straw was his final few weeks at his job—his last three paychecks bounced because the company didn't have the funds to pay him.

Sound hopeless?

It could have been. But something changed for Stephen—and it's the same kind of thing that can change for you. He went back to the drawing board.

Stephen's biggest paradigm shift was realizing the difference between saving and investing: *saving* is putting your money where there is little risk of losing it. *Investing* is putting your money where you might lose it all.

Stephen also wanted to grow his money while protecting it from taxes. He finally found the solution he was looking for: an IUL. He took what little money he received from his tax refund and started a policy. Despite the terrible economic situation, it changed his entire outlook.

In his own words: "I could create a crystal-clear picture of what my financial future would look like. I could have money in case of emergency or capital in case a good investment opportunity came up. I could use my cash value to pay for vacations, get out of debt and send my kids to college or pay for my retirement.

An IUL gave me a sense of security and gratification, knowing that my money would grow and be available for my use and that my family would be protected and taken care of in case something should happen to me. I have an idea of what my future will look like, I know how much money I will have at certain milestones in my life, and I have a strong financial foundation on which to continue building."

Doris Christopher

Doris Christopher may not be a name you recognize, but the company she founded is. Doris was a successful home economist and educator—but she had a dream. All those hours working with homemakers had convinced her that women needed quality timesaving tools designed to make cooking quick and easy. Women didn't want to spend hours and hours in the kitchen grinding out meals—they wanted to create great meals, quickly, due to their increasingly busy schedules.

Doris not only had a dream; she had a plan.

Doris's plan involved an army of consultants who would do in-home cooking demonstrations using her professional-quality tools and equipment. Tupperware had done it, and with outstanding success—a homemaker schedules a party, invites her friends and the rest fell into place.

With the support of her husband, Jay, and that of her two young daughters, Doris came up with a detailed business plan and got ready to put it into action. The only thing standing between her and her dream was money.

Her solution was simple. In 1980, Doris borrowed $3,000 from her life insurance policy, and The Pampered Chef® was born in the basement of her suburban Chicago home.

In the ensuing decades, the business moved to a series of progressively larger facilities. By 2002, the company had blossomed into a $700 million enterprise that was acquired by Warren Buffett's Berkshire Hathaway Corporation. Today, The Pampered Chef® has grown into an international corporation serving 12 million customers annually—and it all started with the loan from her life insurance policy.[34]

Angie

To protect her privacy, we won't tell you Angie's last name—but life insurance agent, Rocky, is happy to tell a convincing story about another aspect of the IUL: the legacy we leave to our family when we pass on.

Angie was married to Michael—a 41-year-old anesthesiologist. They were referred to Rocky by another physician, and Rocky met Angie and Michael at their home to discuss their needs. They had a young family—three children under the age of seven. Together they determined they needed $2 million in life insurance coverage.

After a second meeting, during which Michael filled out all of the applications, Rocky also signed him up for $10,000 a month in disability insurance.

Everything went well for the next 18 months. Suddenly, Michael started getting sick. His weight plummeted. He became so weak that it was a struggle to work. A battery of tests revealed no cause for his medical problems, and he became desperate. Almost out of options, he finally talked to a colleague who suggested a latex allergy as the possible culprit. Michael was tested, and sure enough, he was allergic to latex. His allergic reaction was behind the host of symptoms that had plagued him.

With a confirmed latex allergy, Michael had to stop working in the hospital. His disability insurance kicked in, providing an income of $10,000 a month. Yearning to still practice medicine, Michael used some of his disability income and part of his cash value life policy to start a pain clinic—a clinic with a strict ban on latex of any kind.

Things went very well for two years. One night Angie went out to dinner with friends. Michael, who wasn't feeling well, stayed home. That night, Angie found him dead on the bathroom floor. The autopsy results revealed that Michael had contracted bacterial meningitis—and because of the impact that his latex allergy had on his immune system, he didn't have the ability to fight the infection. It killed powerfully and suddenly.

Shortly thereafter, Rocky delivered a $2 million check to Angie—the amount of the death benefit on the cash value life policy she and Michael had purchased just a few years earlier. Nothing can bring Michael back, but Rocky felt a great sense of satisfaction in helping provide a strong financial future for Angie and her children as a result of their life insurance policy.

Ray Kroc

Ray Kroc came from humble beginnings. Born in Chicago in 1902, at the age of 15, he lied about his age and landed himself a job as an ambulance driver for the Red Cross. Later he actually trained to become an ambulance driver during World War I (where he struck up a friendship with Walt Disney, who was in the same training). Peace treaties were signed before he saw any combat action, so he returned home and tried his hand at a number of jobs—paper-cup salesman, pianist, jazz musician, band member and radio disk jockey. In a move that would later prove fortuitous, Ray worked at a restaurant in exchange for room and board so he could learn the restaurant business.

In 1954, at the age of 52, as a milkshake machine salesman, Ray took notice of a hamburger stand in San Bernardino, California. While most restaurants bought one or two Prince Castle Multi-mixers, which could each mix five shakes at once, the San Bernardino restaurant had bought eight. Curiosity got the better of Ray Kroc, and he wanted to see what kind of restaurant needed to churn forty milkshakes at a time. And so he set out for California.

What Kroc saw when he got to that restaurant—a hamburger stand owned by Maurice and Richard McDonald—would not only change his life forever, but would change the scene of the fast-food industry throughout the world.

Kroc saw the two legendary golden arches and saw lines of people queued up for the restaurant's simple fare of burgers, fries and milkshakes.

Ray Kroc wanted to slow down as a traveling salesman. His health was declining. He was suffering from diabetes and arthritis, and he had bigger fish to fry. Ray managed to convince the brothers to sell the McDonalds name and trade secrets to him, and worked a deal to pay for it with a percentage of the receipts.

McDonald's was on its way to becoming a household name. In 1955, Ray opened his first McDonald's drive-in restaurant in Des Plaines, Illinois.

While things inside the restaurants ran smoothly, Ray faced massive challenges with cash flow, franchises, competition and the economy in general. He was determined to be successful and spent year after year, working day and night, to build his company.

In order to build the largest fast food chain in the world and overcome constant cash-flow problems, Ray took out loans on two cash value life insurance policies to get his infant company off the ground. He used some of the money to create an enduring advertising campaign that centered on the company's mascot, Ronald McDonald.

Ray Kroc passed away from old age in January 1984 at the age of 81, just 10 months before McDonald's sold its fifty-billionth hamburger. At the time of his death there were some 7,500 McDonald's restaurants worldwide. Today, with more than 25,000 restaurants worldwide, McDonald's is the world's largest food-service retailer. With operations in more than 65 countries.

The Wrap

What did you learn from James Cash Penney, Doctor Jeff, Walt Disney, Stephen G., Doris Christopher, Angie and Ray Kroc?

There are important lessons in every one of these examples. You can work as hard as humanly possible. You can make all the right plans. But when the financial storms come, if you have a weak financial foundation it can be devastating. But, if you have the right financial foundation in place, you can withstand them. By having the foundation of a cash value insurance policy in place, you can keep your money safely growing outside of the market. You can have the peace of mind you are looking for.

And here's the really great news. It's not hard or complicated. You don't have to know it all.

To see a personalized blueprint of how an IUL could work for you and your unique situation, just use the form in the back of this book or go to www.wealthbeyondwallstreet.com and fill out a Blueprint Analysis request, and a Wealth Beyond Wall Street professional will work with you to design a custom policy for you and your family—*at no cost.*

This blueprint can show you how to build a sturdy foundation by helping you get out of debt, save on taxes and eliminate the risk of losing your money in the stock market. By creating this firm foundation, you can Finance Yourself to Wealth™ and control your financial future.

Remember what you learned from Aristotle in the opening pages of this book: "Money is a guarantee that we may have what we want in the future."

You may not be able to go back in time and change your beginning, but you can start today and make a brand new ending.

Chapter 12

BONUS CHAPTER: FOR BUSINESS OWNERS ONLY

"The entrepreneur is our visionary, the creator in each of us. We're born with that quality and it defines our lives as we respond to what we see, hear, feel, and experience."

— Michael Gerber

If there's a portion of the country that is underserved and underappreciated it might just be the small business owner.

I know firsthand because I have been one for the better part of a decade and my family has a long genealogy of small business owners.

It goes all the way back to my great, great grandfather who was a watchmaker on Jersey Isle in England.

From there we have my great grandfather who owned a painting construction business, my grandfather who has run multiple businesses and my father who built the largest boat trailer manufacturing company in the mountain west area.

Being a business owner is tough.

I know what it's like to have the stress of overhead, payroll, advertising to get new clients, economic forces outside of our control, the late hours, missed soccer games and the huge amount of risk we take on. We do it all because we want to provide financial security for our families and live the American Dream of financial success.

Most of us don't get benefit packages that someone else is paying for. Usually no one is contributing to *our* retirement plan. We don't punch a time clock or have the luxury of having someone else cut us a check every two weeks.

It's common knowledge that the small business owner is the engine of the American economy. Yet too often we work ourselves to death, and continually pour any extra money back into the business, often neglecting our own savings as we try to build our companies.

If you are anything like me, we approach our business with a case of never ending faith that next week, month or year we'll make the money we want. And soon months and years have passed, and we've invested everything back into the business and haven't stashed anything away for ourselves.

Joining the ranks of the wealthy beyond Wall Street could change that right now.

Not only can an IUL create an "automatic wealth building machine" where you put money away each month without thinking about it, but you can still access that money for use *in* your business.

Let's talk about three simple ways you can be using an IUL to save money, prepare for the future and help your business grow.

Finance Yourself to Wealth™

If you buy equipment, vehicles or own real estate for your business or investments, this is for you.

Funding an IUL can be done a couple different ways.

You can start by simply putting in a set amount of money each month, then borrowing against that cash value to buy whatever you need for your business.

You can also start a policy by dumping in a one-time payment like $20,000, $50,000 or even $100,000 and using that as your own source of funding. It's kind of like your own private source of financing, except no qualifying is necessary to use the cash!

Use your IUL to buy business equipment, vehicles or real estate by using the money in your policy while it still grows as if you've never touched it.

Instead of going out and buying a truck for your company the old way, use your policy to finance your purchase, then recoup the cost of the truck by paying your insurance loan back.

You can even get more advanced by using these policies as a separate entity that acts as a leasing company that purchases vehicles, real estate and other equipment.

If the Worst Should Happen

Ever heard of a business getting destroyed because a partner dies and the spouse comes in to take over the interest with no experience whatsoever?

I really do like my business partner's wife, but she and I running a business together would not be a pretty picture.

It happens more often than you might think.

In fact, take a look at these sobering statistics.

These figures show the likelihood, out of 100, that one of two business partners in good health will die prior to 65:

Age of Business Owner	Chances
40/40	35%
45/45	33%
50/50	29.9%
55/55	24.7%

If there are three partners, the percentages are much higher.[35]

So what does that mean for you and your business? If you have a partner, or two, you can use an IUL insurance policy to fund a buy-sell agreement. This would provide you with cash to buy out that partner's ownership of the business if they should die. The company can continue to thrive without the disruption of a new partner and the spouse of the partner will be compensated fairly.

But it gets even better than that.

Let's go for the best-case scenario. Assume you and your partner both live long healthy lives.

You get to enjoy all the living benefits of the IUL throughout your lives the same way we already have described previously. Use it for vehicle financing, major purchases, funding growth or buying real estate.

Ride Off into the Sunset

This is ultimately where you probably want to be.

We've hopefully already established in black and white why a solid financial foundation is the key to a great lifestyle— but why not use this powerful tool to grow your business, save you money on interest throughout your life, and then enjoy a passive stream of cash flow that comes from your policy as you travel to exotic destinations with your spouse, golfing the days away and enjoying the fruits that you worked so hard for.

> "The single biggest benefit in the tax code is the tax exemption for life insurance."
> —Ed Slott,
> The Retirement
> Savings Time Bomb

If all the living benefits weren't enough to convince you that an IUL should be a part of your financial plan, this might.

Willie Sutton and the Tax Man always follow the money.

Estate taxes can be over 50% of your estate, and that's not just liquid funds. It could include residential and commercial real estate, investments and all the assets you may have. Often people underestimate their estates, and yet they can add up to $800,000 to $1,000,000 fairly quickly.

Imagine the problem your family could have when they get a tax bill saying they owe $500,000 and much of that is tied up in real estate.

This is especially problematic if the real estate market is down, and people have to "fire sell" at below market value just to satisfy the demands of the tax man.

Here's where the IUL really shines.

Under current IRS tax code, life insurance proceeds are paid out income tax free. This means they come to the estate or your family (depending on how the policies are set up) in a lump sum. You can use that money to pay the estate taxes, while protecting your other hard earned assets.

Life insurance payouts *are* usually subject to estate taxes, so keep that in mind when you calculate how much insurance you'll need to cover the entire tax bill…and as always, consult with a proper estate tax planning professional.

This is where a Wealth Beyond Wall Street professional could really help you. Not only can they help you with an IUL but also with asset protection, estate tax planning, and other issues to help build a strategy for protecting and growing your wealth. Just go to www.wealthbeyondwallstreet.com to request a free Blueprint for Business Owners Only. A professional who has gone through an extensive amount of training on structuring these policies can help you achieve all your goals now to protect your legacy.

ACKNOWLEDGEMENTS

I never imagined how incredibly happy I would be writing this page…knowing that the book is complete.

Writing a book while running two companies and being husbands, fathers, and bosses has not been an easy task.

We're hoping it will provide hope and a clear path to becoming financially independent.

First, we would like to thank our wives and kids for putting up with never ending work hours, stresses beyond our imagination, and supporting us through it all.

Thanks to editors who proofread and cleaned up the important content we wanted to share with the world. It's been a big job!

We also want to thank our Wealth Beyond Wall Street professionals who are helping families across the country become financially independent! Your support and work changes lives.

Thank you.

Free Bonus Content

27 Second Retirement Calculator

Discover how long your retirement savings will last based on your current situation.

Wealth Beyond Wall Street Toolkit

Get our videos, analysis and wealth comparison checklist.

Free Blueprint Analysis

Talk with a trained professional who can show you in black and white how to create the financial independence you are looking for.

Lifestyle Income Calculator

Discover how long your income will last living the lifestyle you want.

Finance Yourself To Wealth Video Series

Discover the power of reducing or eliminating interest you pay to banks and credit card companies.

Wealth Beyond Wall Street For Business Owners

See how the IUL can protect your business, build your wealth and save taxes.

FREE Monthly Online Training Events!

Join our online trainings to speed up your path to wealthy beyond Wall Street status!

All on www.wealthbeyondwallstreet.com

Confidential Blueprint Analysis
Use Black Ink Please

Name: _____

Address: _____

City, State and Zip: _____

Primary Email Address: _____

Cell Phone:_____Evening Phone: _____

Best time to reach you: _____

Were you referred by anyone? _____

Please rate your priorities from 1 to 5 **being the most important:**

_____Having an income for life

_____Keeping your money safely growing outside the market

_____Fast access to your money…on your terms

_____Getting out of debt

_____Financing Yourself To Wealth

To best prepare to help you, please tell us about yourself:

Age:_____

Occupation: _____

Income: _____

Do you own your home? Yes or No

Years left on Mortgage?_____ Balance on Mortgage?_____

Do you own a business? _____

IMPORTANT: Your information is accessed by a Wealth Beyond Wall Street professional so they can provide your analysis. We ask for your phone and email to be able to provide your Blueprint analysis to you. Your Wealth Beyond Wall Street professional will design a custom Blueprint that may help you reach your financial goals. By filling out and returning this form you are giving us permission to contact you.

How to request your Blueprint Analysis:

1. **Return this form by mail to Wealth Education Group, 7410 So. Creek Rd, Suite 203, Sandy, UT 84093**

2. **Fax this form to 801-693-1674**

3. **Request a blueprint through our website at www.wealthbeyondwallstreet.com**

ENDNOTES

1. Federal Reserve Board, 2004

2. Cardweb.com

3. 60 minutes, 401(k) Recession, Ira Rosen

4. *US News and World Report*; 7 Retirement Risks You Need To Prepare for, April 2, 2010. Emily Brandon

5. *Become Your Own Banker*, 2008, Nelson Nash

6. FDIC.gov; Foreclosure statistics

7. AFL-CIO analysis of 292 companies in the S&P 500 Index. CEO pay data provided by salary.com.

8. Barry James Dyke, *Pirates of Manhattan*

9. Nelson Nash, *Becoming Your Own Banker*

10. Barry James Dyke, *Pirates of Manhattan*

11. http://www.davemanuel.com/inflation-calculator.php

12. http://business.time.com/2013/03/12/if-theres-no-inflation-why-are-prices-up-so-much/

13. http://news.bbc.co.uk/2/hilbusiness/3746044.stm, Monday, 1 November, 2004, news.bbc.co.uk

14. http://www.kiplinger.com/magazine/archives/2008105/hidden-401(k)-fees.html#ixzz13CwvXJKI

15. Damien Hoffman, *Cramer Buy Recommendation CIT Goes Bankrupt*, Wall St. Cheat Sheet, Nov. 1, 2009.

16. Bill Alpert, *Cramer :S Star Outshines His Stock Picks*, Baron :S , Feb. 9, 2009.

17. Ira Rosen, *The 401(k) Fallout*, 60 Minutes

18. FBI History, Famous Cases, Willie Sutton, www.jbi.gov

19. http://wwwjorbes.com/forbes/201010426/investing-obama-tax-hikes-capital-gains-duck-obamatax.htmI

20. Scott Shultz, www.avoidthedeferraltrap.com

21. Becoming Your Own Banker, Nelson Nash

22. William Wolman and Anne Colamosca, *The Great 401(k) Hoax: Why Your Family's Financial Security Is at Risk and What You Can Do About It* (Cambridge, MA: Perseus Publishing, 2002), 12.

23. *The Outer Limits, Some of These Funds Go Way Beyond the Ordinary*, Forbes, September 18, 2006.

24. Anthony Mirhaydari, *MSN Money*. The following adapted from Barry James Dyke, *The Pirates of Manhattan: Systematically Plundering the American Consumer and How to Protect Against It* (Hampton, NH: 555 Publishing, Inc., 2008), 69-76.

25. http://www.miravast.com/Images/BH_Miravast_LSR_07192013.pdf

26. http://www.livinghistoryfarm.org

27. http://blogs.wsj.com/deals/2010111108/tracking-bank-failures-2010-tops-2009-for-bank-failures/

28. *Pirates of Manhattan*, Barry James Dyke

29. Ed Slott, *The Retirement Savings Time Bomb ... and How to Diffuse It*.

30. In the event of a lapse, outstanding policy loans in excess of unrecovered cost basis will be subject to ordinary income tax. Tax laws are subject to change. Be sure to consult a tax professional beforehand.

31. Based on illustration of 42 year old male, preferred health, using an A Rated Indexed Life Insurance Company illustration using a 5.0% variable loan rate and 7.5% monthly growth cap.

32. http:l/.finance.yahoo.com/focus-retirement/article/110176/ predicting-your-life-expectancy?mod=fidelity readytoretire&cat=fidelity_2010_getting_ready_to_retire

33. Adapted from Catherine and Richard Greene, *The Man Behind the Magic: The Story of Walt Disney* (NY: Viking Penguin, 1991).

34. (Currency/Doubleday, 2005) and *Come to the Table: A Celebration of Family Life* (Warner Books, 1999).

35. http://www.raricklaw.com/assets/pdf/client-newsroom/20091